TOWN SQUARE
SAMPLER

Eleanor Burns

To the great Townspeople of Quilt in a Day
Thank you for all your help!

Photo on Title Page left to right...

Remi Barranco Distribution
Merritt Voigtlander Art Director
Nancy Petrovich Distribution
Robin Green Production Assistant
Rick Roessler Video Production
Orion Burns General Manager
Pat Wetzel Educator, Sales Associate
Mary Devendorf Customer Service
Andy Devendorf Webmaster
Judy Jackson Customer Service Manager
Judy Holm Customer Service
Gayle Snitselaar Merchandiser
Cindi Weinheimer Retail Store Manager
Teresa Varnes Production Assistance
Sue Bouchard Executive Assistant, Educator
Eleanor Burns Chief Executive Officer
Patricia Knoechel Educator
Dawn Harman Sales Associate
Helen Schelle Sales Associate
Amie Potter Sales Associate
Sunny Schultz Sales Associate
Jean Aloia Educator, Sales Associate
Sheila Meehan Educator, Sales Associate
Anne Dease Educator
Luckie Yasukochi Educator, Sales Associate
Luann Stout Head Teacher
Mary Hawkins Accounting

First printing March, 2000

Published by Quilt in a Day®, Inc.
1955 Diamond St, San Marcos, CA 92069

©2000 by Eleanor A. Burns Family Trust

ISBN 1-891776-01-0

Art Director Merritt Voigtlander
Production Assistant Robin Green

Contents

Welcome to Town Square

I grew up in Zelienople, Pennsylvania, a small town just north of Pittsburgh. I've stitched together such fond memories of that town! There's patches of my family, my friends, teachers from school and church. Their influence is woven through my life. Town Square Sampler pays tribute to those pieces from my past.

Just as my small town celebrates the four seasons, I have stitched quilts to represent each season. The quilt is constructed in rows, with a different technique in each row. They sew up so quickly, you will never get bored! The full size Town Square fits a queen size bed, or you could stitch up blocks from the rows and sew them into smaller projects.

Throughout the Town Square Sampler, I've shared stories of my past. I hope that you too can bring some home town memories alive with your quilting.

Eleanor Burns

4

Fabric Selection

Decide which **season** as Spring, Summer, Fall, or Winter and which theme you wish to portray, as **Contemporary or Country**. Small accents of brighter colors add sparkle to your quilt.

Choose Sky and Ground fabrics for **Spring and Summer** that are non-directional and contrasting with minimal texture.

For **Fall**, you might choose a beige or tan Sky, and light to medium green for the Ground.

For a snowy **Winter** effect, choose a dark blue, starry Sky, and snow white Ground.

Place **patchwork fabrics** against the Sky and Ground fabrics depending on their placement. Look for fabrics that show contrast in color and value. Choose fabrics and colors that can be repeated throughout the quilt to give it continuity.

Select three fabrics for your **Split Rail Border** in one medium and two dark values. Preferably, choose warm and cool colors to show contrast as red, gold, and green.

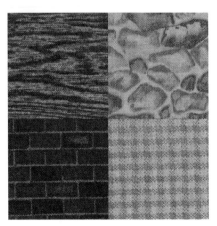

Select Main Street **fabrics with architectural textures** that resemble wood, stones, bricks, stain glass windows, and roof tiles. Checks also make good buildings. For the trees, choose **several greens**.

For added embellishment, you might want to add appliqued birds, flowers, people, or flags to your quilt.

Winter

Winter Carnival   *Sue Bouchard*

Sky

Ground

It's wintertime, and snow covers the Town Square. The blocks of the Winter quilt contrast sharply with a dark blue Sky and white Ground. Patchwork trees surround the buildings of Main Street, and Christmas Angels hold a banner of Celebration over the town. Snuggle under this quilt for a cozy winter's nap.

6

Sky

Ground

Spring Festival   *Patricia Knoechel*

Springtime blooms with fresh colors and a garland of silk flowers. Fussy cut flower beds brighten Main Street. Look closely and you'll even see fussy cut people in the windows of the School and Cottage. Edna's Pinwheel row appears as a white picket fence in a light floral print. Applique trees and green Maple Leaves soften the springtime scene.

Summer

Sky

Ground

Summer in the Park   *Eleanor Burns*

Summer is here! Sunshine yellow fabric appears throughout the Summer quilt. Clouds float in a gentle blue Sky and the Ground is a rich grass green. One color Maple Leaves glow with deep green of summer, and the Duck and Ducklings Row blooms like a field of flowers. It's a patriotic summer celebration in the old Town Square.

Sky

Ground

Country Fair   *Sandy Thompson*

Fall colors bring back memories of cider and caramel, cinnamon and apples at the Country Fair. An even beige is used for the Sky fabric, suggesting the overcast days of the season. A small Triangle Tree graces a spot beside the Cottage. The Ground beneath the Main Street Row glows with the golden light of autumn. Thanksgiving is just around the corner.

Yardage Chart

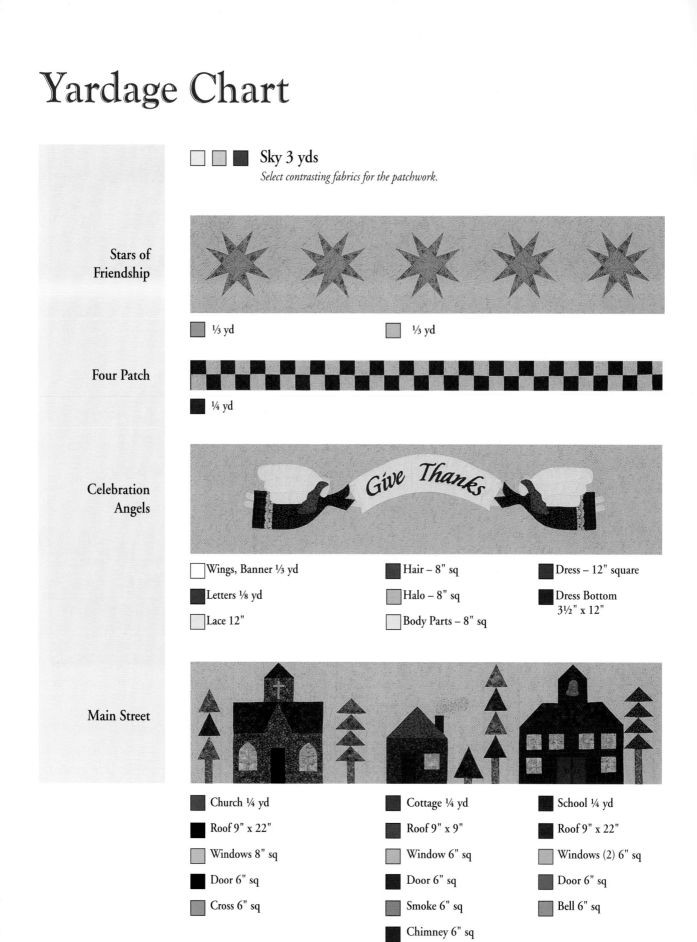

Sky 3 yds
Select contrasting fabrics for the patchwork.

Stars of Friendship

⬜ ⅓ yd   ⬜ ⅓ yd

Four Patch

⬛ ¼ yd

Celebration Angels

⬜ Wings, Banner ⅓ yd   ⬛ Hair – 8" sq   ⬛ Dress – 12" square

⬛ Letters ⅛ yd   ⬜ Halo – 8" sq   ⬛ Dress Bottom 3½" x 12"

⬜ Lace 12"   ⬜ Body Parts – 8" sq

Main Street

⬛ Church ¼ yd   ⬛ Cottage ¼ yd   ⬛ School ¼ yd

⬛ Roof 9" x 22"   ⬛ Roof 9" x 9"   ⬛ Roof 9" x 22"

⬜ Windows 8" sq   ⬜ Window 6" sq   ⬜ Windows (2) 6" sq

⬛ Door 6" sq   ⬛ Door 6" sq   ⬛ Door 6" sq

⬜ Cross 6" sq   ⬜ Smoke 6" sq   ⬜ Bell 6" sq

                       ⬛ Chimney 6" sq

⬛ First Trees ¼ yd   ⬛ Trunks 4½" x 22"   ⬛ Second Trees ¼ yd

10

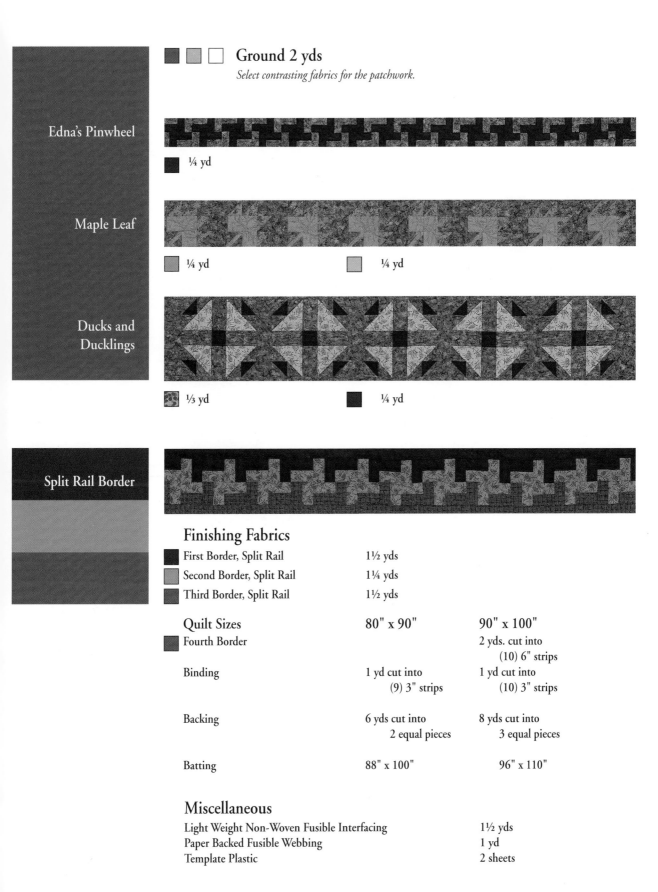

Ground 2 yds
Select contrasting fabrics for the patchwork.

Edna's Pinwheel

¼ yd

Maple Leaf

¼ yd   ¼ yd

Ducks and
Ducklings

⅓ yd   ¼ yd

Split Rail Border

Finishing Fabrics

First Border, Split Rail	1½ yds	
Second Border, Split Rail	1¼ yds	
Third Border, Split Rail	1½ yds	

Quilt Sizes	80" x 90"	90" x 100"
Fourth Border		2 yds. cut into (10) 6" strips
Binding	1 yd cut into (9) 3" strips	1 yd cut into (10) 3" strips
Backing	6 yds cut into 2 equal pieces	8 yds cut into 3 equal pieces
Batting	88" x 100"	96" x 110"

Miscellaneous

Light Weight Non-Woven Fusible Interfacing	1½ yds
Paper Backed Fusible Webbing	1 yd
Template Plastic	2 sheets

Supplies

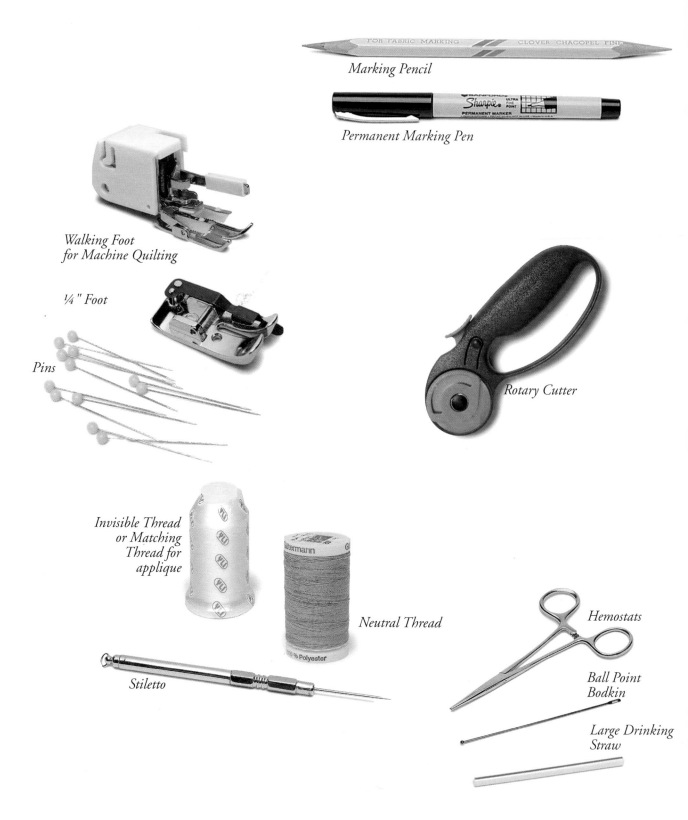

Marking Pencil

Permanent Marking Pen

Walking Foot
for Machine Quilting

¼ " Foot

Pins

Rotary Cutter

Invisible Thread
or Matching
Thread for
applique

Neutral Thread

Stiletto

Hemostats

Ball Point
Bodkin

Large Drinking
Straw

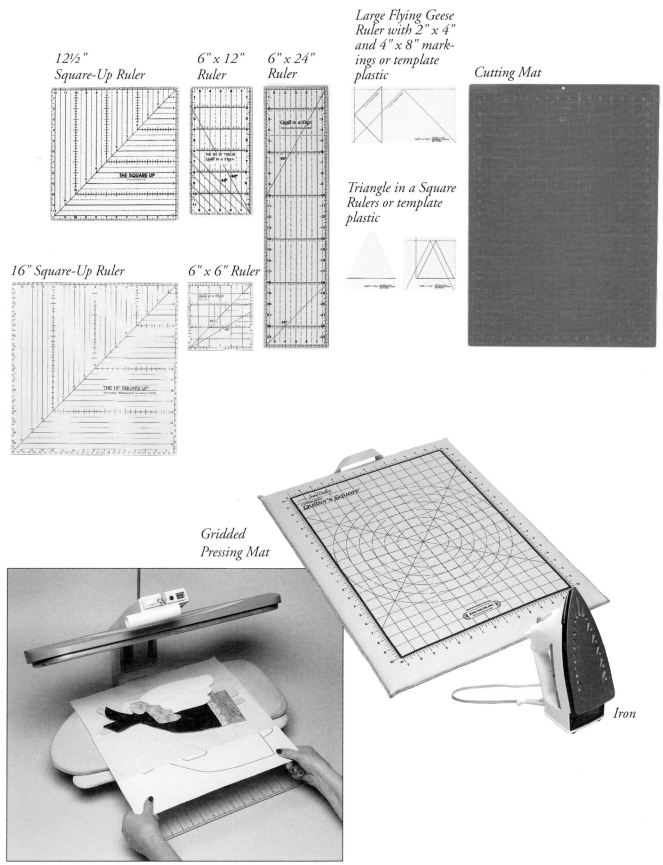

12½"
Square-Up Ruler

6" x 12"
Ruler

6" x 24"
Ruler

Large Flying Geese
Ruler with 2" x 4"
and 4" x 8" mark-
ings or template
plastic

Cutting Mat

16" Square-Up Ruler

6" x 6" Ruler

Triangle in a Square
Rulers or template
plastic

Gridded
Pressing Mat

Iron

Applique Pressing Sheet   Electronic Press Optional

Triangle in a Square Templates

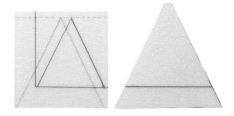

The Triangle in a Square rulers are available on heavy plexiglas from Quilt in a Day. Cutting with these rulers makes the process easier, and cut pieces are more accurate.

If you do not have these rulers, tape template plastic to this page, trace templates with colored sharp markers, and cut out on the outside lines.

When indicated to use Triangle in a Square rulers, trace around the triangle template with a marking pen, and rotary cut on the lines with a 6" x 12" ruler.

Tape the square template to the underneath side of a plexiglas 6" x 6" ruler and use as instructed.

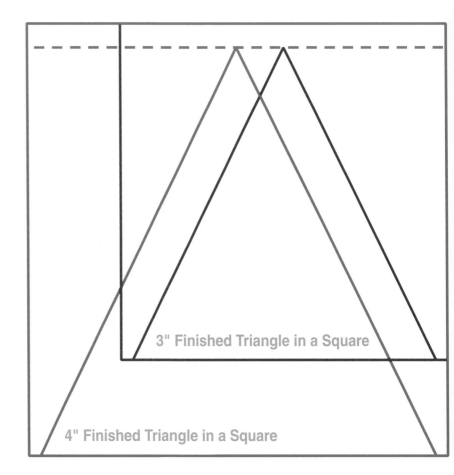

3" Finished Triangle in a Square

4" Finished Triangle in a Square

3" Finished Triangle in a Square

4" Finished Triangle in a Square

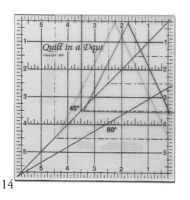

Flying Geese Template

The Large Flying Geese ruler is available on heavy plexiglas from Quilt in a Day. Cutting with this ruler makes the process easier, and cut pieces are more accurate.

If you do not have this ruler, trace the template on template plastic and cut out on the outside lines. Tape the template to the underneath side of a plexiglas 6" x 6" ruler, and use as instructed.

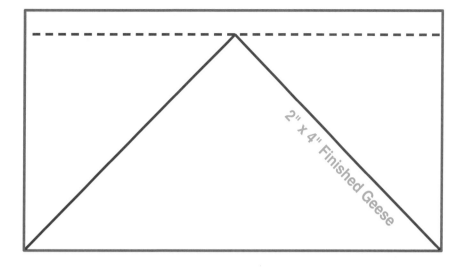

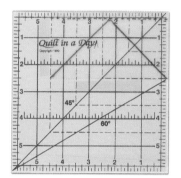

Cutting Strips Selvage to Selvage

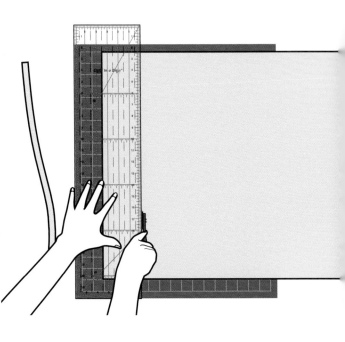

1. Cut a nick in one selvage, the tightly woven edge on both sides of the fabric. Tear across the grain from selvage to selvage.

2. Press the fabric, particularly the torn edge.

3. Fold the fabric in half, matching the frayed edges. Don't worry about the selvages not lining up correctly as this is not always possible. Line up the straight of the grain.

4. Place the fabric on the gridded mat with the folded edge along a horizontal line, and the torn edge on a vertical line.

5. Place the quarter inch line of the ruler along the torn edge of the fabric.

6. Spread your fingers and place four on top of the ruler with the little finger on the edge to keep the ruler firmly in place.

7. Take the rotary cutter in your free hand and open the blade. Starting below the fabric, begin cutting away from you, applying pressure on the ruler and the cutter. Keep the blade next to the ruler's edge. Cut off the torn edge.

8. Cut strips according to the yardage chart. Open the first strip and look at the fold to see if it is straight. If it has a crook that looks like an elbow, the fabric may not be folded on the straight of the grain. If this happens repeat the preceding steps.

Sample Set of Cutting Instructions

Specific cutting instructions are given with each row. You may prefer to cut pieces prior to sewing each row, or cut all pieces before starting to sew. Each set of instructions lists fabrics to use and the pieces to cut from those fabrics. This is a sample set with explanation.

Ground

(3) 2½" strips cut into
    (8) 2½" squares
    (9) 2½" x 6½"

Window

(1) 8" square

1. From Ground fabric, cut (3) 2½" strips selvage to selvage with 6" x 24" ruler.

2. Place folded strips straight on grid. Square off selvage edges.

3. Place 6" square ruler on strip with #1 in upper right hand corner. Place 2½" squaring line on cut edge. Layer cut toward the fold (8) 2½" squares.

4. With 6" x 12" ruler, cut remainder of 2½" strips into (9) 2½" x 6½" pieces.

5. Place Window fabric on cutting mat. Place 12½" square ruler on fabric with #1 in upper right hand corner, and at least ½" extra fabric past 8" square.

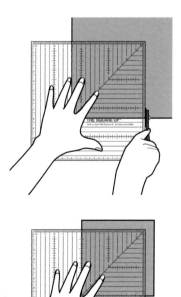

6. Cut fabric on right side of ruler and across top.

7. Lift ruler and turn piece of fabric 90 degrees. **Do not turn the ruler.**

8. Place 8" squaring lines on cut edge, and repeat cutting.

General Sewing

Sewing Techniques

Use a fine, sharp, #70/10 needle. Use small stitches, approximately 15 per inch, or 2.0 on computer machines with stitch selections from 1 to 4. When sewing through batting, use a machine quilting needle and 10 stitches per inch or 3.5 on a computer machine.

¼" Seam Allowance Test

Use a consistent ¼" seam allowance throughout the construction of the quilt. If necessary, adjust the needle position, change the presser foot, or feed the fabric under the presser foot to achieve the ¼". **Complete the ¼" seam allowance test before starting.**

1. Cut (3) 1½" x 6" pieces, and sew the three strips together lengthwise with what you **think** is a ¼" seam.

2. Press the seams in one direction. Make sure no folds occur at the seams when pressing.

3. Place the sewn sample under a ruler and measure its width. It should measure exactly 3½". If sample measures smaller than 3½", seam is too large. If sample measures larger than 3½", seam is too small. Adjust the seam allowance and repeat if necessary.

¼" Foot

Available for most sewing machines, the ¼" foot has a guide on it to help you keep your fabric from straying, giving you perfect ¼" seams. Your patchwork is then consistently accurate.

Neutral Thread

Sew the quilt blocks together with a good quality polyester or cotton spun thread in a neutral shade. When machine quilting, use the same color thread as the backing in the bobbin. Use regular or invisible thread on the top.

Pressing

Throughout the quilt construction, it is important to set the seams, or lock the stitches, and then press the seams in a given direction.

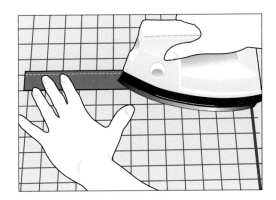

1. Before opening, lay the sewn strips or pieces on the gridded pressing mat. Line up strips with the grid to avoid "bowing." Place the strip on top that you want the seam directed to.

2. Press the strips to set the seam. The use of steam is your preference.

3. Lift the upper strip and press toward the fold. The seam will naturally fall behind the upper strip. Check that there are no folds at the seam line.

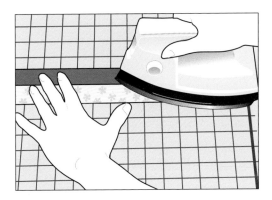

4. Turn the strips over. Check that the seams are pressed in the right direction.

Locking Seams

A general rule is to press the seams to the darkest side. However, some pieces have locking seams, so they may not follow that rule.

Pressing Flat Pieces

Pieces as the Geese and Triangle in a Square are pressed in the direction of least resistance so they lay flat. Follow the instructions for which way to press.

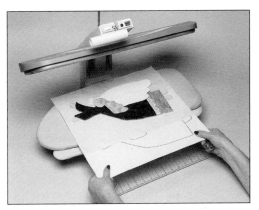

Use an electronic press to fuse applique pieces.

Four Patch and Edna's Pinwheel Rows

Aunt Edna's Quilt, *Page 124*

Edna Scheidemantle

Erma and Erwin Knoechel

My Mom, Erma Drushel, loved to spend time with her Aunt Edna Scheidemantle, who lived on a farm and raised chickens, among other animals. She met my father, Erwin Knoechel, while at Edna's farm. Maybe my mom planned it!

To Father's dismay, Mother had four daughters in a row - her little Four Patches! Peace finally came to the Knoechel house when Baby Bruce came along!

We all grew up loving Aunt Edna! She generously shared her chicken feed sacks for my first sewing projects.

Cutting for Sixteen Four Patches

▬ Fall _____

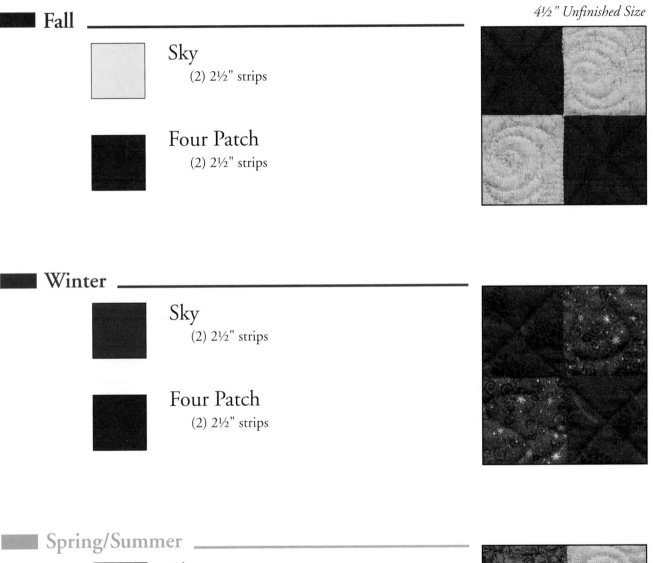

Sky
(2) 2½" strips

Four Patch
(2) 2½" strips

▬ Winter _____

Sky
(2) 2½" strips

Four Patch
(2) 2½" strips

▬ Spring/Summer _____

Sky
(2) 2½" strips

Four Patch
(2) 2½" strips

Making Sixteen Four Patches *Illustrations match Fall color code.*

1. Sew 2½" Sky and Four Patch strips right sides together. Use an accurate ¼" seam.

2. Set seams with Four Patch strip on top, open, and press against seam.

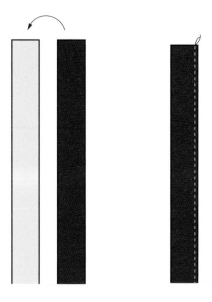

3. Measure width of strips. They should measure 4½". Adjust the seam if necessary.

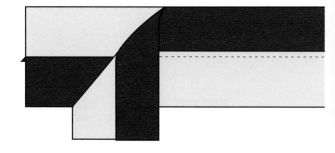

4. Layer first strip right side up on gridded cutting mat with Sky across top. Place second strip right sides together to it with Four Patch across top. Lock seams. Line up strips with grid.

5. Square left end. Cut (16) 2½" pairs. Stack on spare ruler to carry to sewing area.

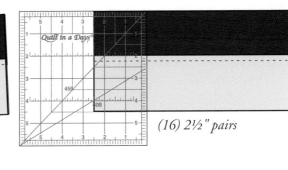

(16) 2½" pairs

6. Matching outside edges and center seam, assembly-line sew. Use stiletto to hold outside edges together and seams flat.

7. Repeat with all pieces.

8. Set seams with last stitching across top, open, and press against seam. Carefully stack in same order.

Sewing Row Together

1. Divide into two piles of eight blocks.

2. Turn so center seam on left stack goes down, and center seam in right stack goes up.

3. Flip top block right sides together to block on left, lock center seams, and match outside edges. Assembly-line sew.

4. Clip apart, stack into two piles, and continue to sew pairs together into one row.

5. Press seams to one side.

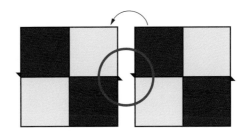

Approximate Finished Length: 4½" x 64½".
This row determines the length of all the rows.

Cutting for Sixteen Pinwheels

■ Fall

4½" Unfinished Size

Ground

Block
  (5) 1½" strips

Row Ends
  (2) 2½" x 4½" rectangles

Row Divider
  (2) 2½" strips

Pinwheel

Block
  (5) 1½" strips

■ Winter

Ground

Block
  (5) 1½" strips

Row Ends
  (2) 2½" x 4½" rectangles

Row Divider
  (2) 2½" strips

Pinwheel

Block
  (5) 1½" strips

■ Spring/Summer

Ground

Block
  (5) 1½" strips

Row Ends
  (2) 2½" x 4½" rectangles

Row Divider
  (2) 2½" strips

Pinwheel

Block
  (5) 1½" strips

Making Sixteen Pinwheels *Illustrations match Fall color code.*

1. Sew 1½" Ground and Pinwheel strips right sides together. Use an accurate ¼" seam.

2. Set seams with darkest strip on top, open, and press against seam.

3. Measure width of strips. They should measure 2½". Make an adjustment in your seam allowance if necessary.

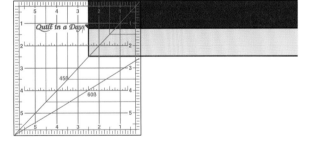

4. Layer strips right sides up on gridded cutting mat. Square left end.

5. Cut (64) 2½" pieces.

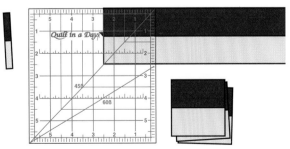

(64) 2½" pieces

6. Divide into four stacks with 16 in each. Turn pieces with Pinwheel meeting in the center.

7. Flip top pieces right sides together to pieces on left.

Place Pinwheel strips meeting in the center with Ground on the outside.

8. Matching outside edges, assembly-line sew. Use stiletto to pull outside edges together and hold seams flat.

9. Repeat with all pieces.

10. Clip apart every other pair. Open.

11. Flip right sides together, pushing top center seam down, and underneath center seam up.

12. Assembly-line sew, holding seams flat with stiletto.

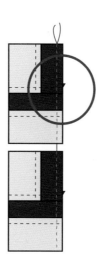

13. Set seams, open, and press against seam. Carefully stack in same order.

14. Divide into two piles of eight blocks.

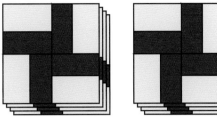

Sewing Row Together

1. Turn so center seam on left stack goes down, and center seam in right stack goes up.

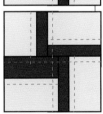

2. Flip top block right sides together to block on left, lock center seams, and match outside edges. Assembly-line sew.

3. Clip apart, stack into two piles, and sew pairs together into one row.

4. Measure against the Four Patch Row. If Edna's Pinwheel Row is shorter, sew 2½" x 4½" Ground rectangles to each end.

5. Press seams away from Pinwheels.

6. Sew 2½" Ground strips into one long strip. Sew to bottom of row.

7. Press seam away from Pinwheel.

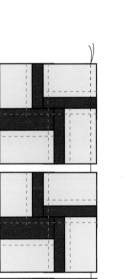

Approximate Finished Length: 64½"
Row will be trimmed later to match the other rows.

2½" x 4½"
Ground
Rectangles

2½" Strip

2½" x 4½"
Ground
Rectangles

Maple Leaf Row

Fall Harvest, *Page 130*

Maple Leaf Curtains, *Page 128*

Left to right -
Kathy, Eleanor, Patty

We planted a maple tree outside our
kitchen window when we first moved in
Grandview Ave. As we grew, so did the tr
It was our friend, offering us shade in the
summer while we played with our dolls.
the fall, we'd rake the beautiful leaves in
paths, and chase each other around the
yard! Our Maple Tree was a welcomed
sight, day after day!

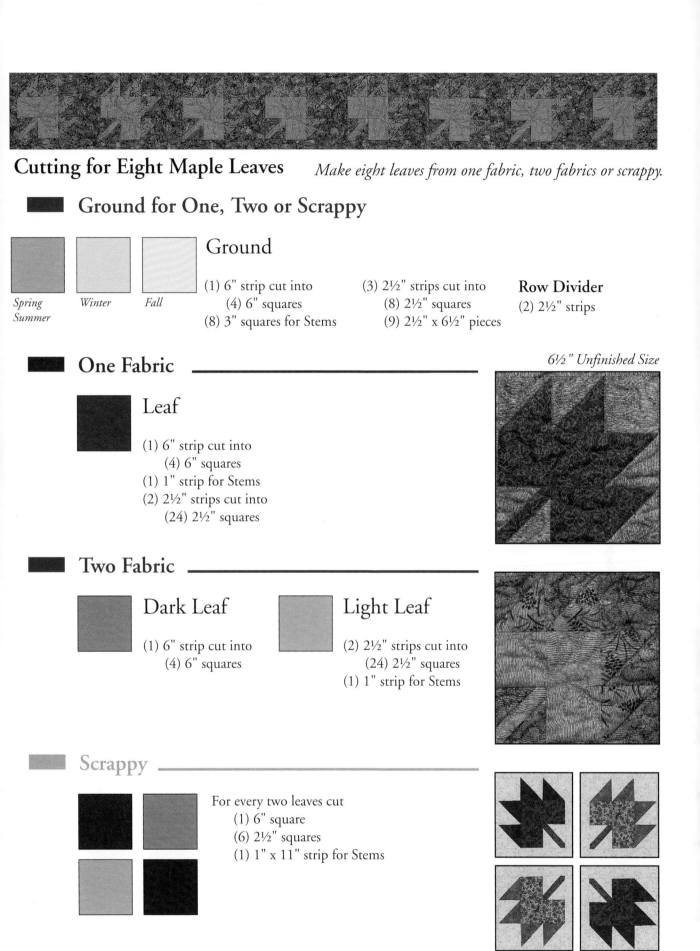

Cutting for Eight Maple Leaves

Make eight leaves from one fabric, two fabrics or scrappy.

▮ Ground for One, Two or Scrappy

Ground

Spring Summer *Winter* *Fall*

(1) 6" strip cut into
    (4) 6" squares
    (8) 3" squares for Stems

(3) 2½" strips cut into
    (8) 2½" squares
    (9) 2½" x 6½" pieces

Row Divider
(2) 2½" strips

▮ One Fabric ————————————

6½" Unfinished Size

Leaf

(1) 6" strip cut into
    (4) 6" squares
(1) 1" strip for Stems
(2) 2½" strips cut into
    (24) 2½" squares

▮ Two Fabric ————————————

Dark Leaf

(1) 6" strip cut into
    (4) 6" squares

Light Leaf

(2) 2½" strips cut into
    (24) 2½" squares
(1) 1" strip for Stems

▮ Scrappy ————————————

For every two leaves cut
    (1) 6" square
    (6) 2½" squares
    (1) 1" x 11" strip for Stems

Making Triangle Pieced Squares

1. Place four 6" squares Ground right sides together to four 6" squares Dark Leaf. Place the lightest fabric on top, wrong side up. Press.

2. Draw two diagonal lines, corner to corner. Pin.

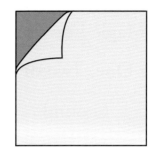 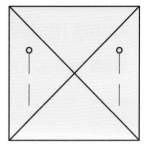

3. Continuously sew an accurate ¼" from one diagonal line. Turn the squares and sew ¼" on opposite side of diagonal line, until you get back to where you started.

4. Clip squares apart.

5. Sew ¼" from both sides of second diagonal line.

6. Press to set seams.

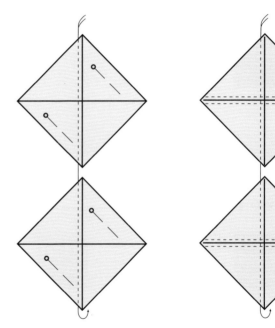

7. Place on gridded cutting mat. Using the lines on the mat and ruler, cut into 3" squares.

8. Cut on diagonal lines.

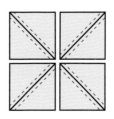 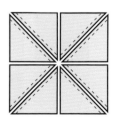

9. Place on pressing mat with Leaf fabric on top, open, and press against seam.

Squaring Up to 2½"

1. Place 6" Square Up ruler on patch so 2½" is centered, and diagonal line on ruler matches seam. Trim on two sides.

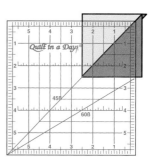

2. Turn patch and place 2½" line on cut edges. Cut remaining two sides, squaring patch to 2½".

3. Make four stacks with eight in each.

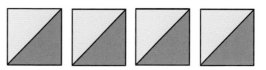

If making scrappy leaves, layer so fabrics are beside each other.

Making Stem Patch

1. Cut 3" Ground squares in half on one diagonal.

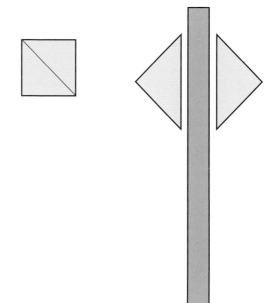

2. Make two equal stacks, right side up, with 1" Stem strip.

3. Flip Ground triangle on right to Stem strip, and sew.

4. Leave 1" space, and sew second triangle. Repeat for all triangles in right stack.

5. Set seams with Stem on top, open and press against seam.

6. Carefully center second triangle on first triangle. Assembly-line sew.

7. Set seam with Stem on top, open, and press against seam.

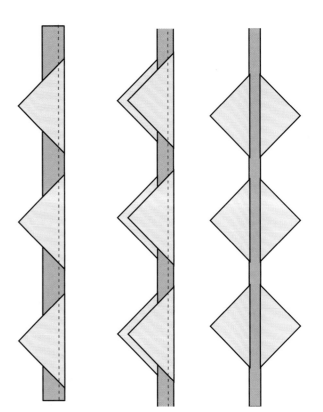

8. Cut apart in 1" spaces.

9. Square to 2½", carefully centering ruler's diagonal line on Stem.

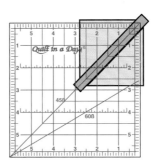

Sewing Block Together

1. Lay out Stems, Triangle Pieced Squares, 2½" Ground and 2½" Medium squares. Place eight in each stack.

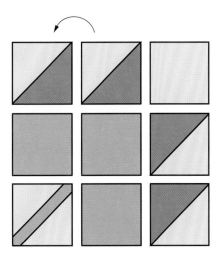

2. Flip second vertical row right sides together to first vertical row.

3. Matching outside edges, assembly-line sew. Use stiletto to hold seams flat. **Do not clip apart.**

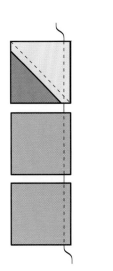
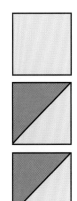

4. Flip third vertical row to second vertical row, and assembly-line sew.

5. Clip apart after every third piece.

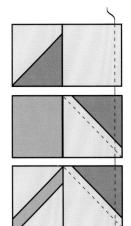

6. Flip right row onto middle row.

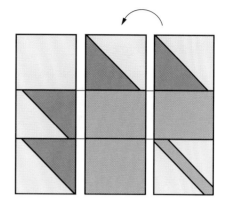

7. Fingerpress and match top seams up, and underneath seams down. Assembly-line sew.

8. Flip middle row right sides together to last row. Fingerpress and match top seams down, and underneath seams up. Assembly-line sew.

9. Press seams away from Stem on the wrong side.

10. Measure. Blocks should measure 6½" square.

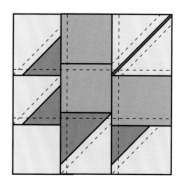

Sewing Row Together

1. Make two stacks of four Maple Leaves. Place with two stacks of four 2½" x 6½" Ground strips.

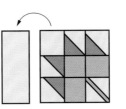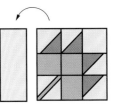

Place four in each stack.

2. Flip Leaf right sides together to strip. Assembly-line sew.

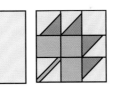

3. Set seams with strip on top, open, and press toward strip.

4. Sew eight Leaves together into one row.

5. Sew remaining 2½" x 6½" strip to right end. Press seams toward strips.

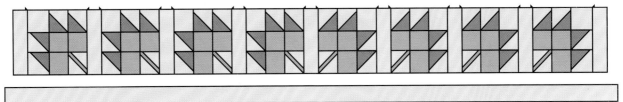

Leaves are pointing half and half.

6. Sew 2½" Ground strips into one long strip. Pin and sew to bottom of Leaves. Trim ends even.

7. Press seam away from Leaves.

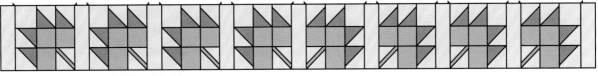

Approximate Finished Length: 66½". Leaf Row will be trimmed later to match other rows.

Ducks and Ducklings or Grandmother's Choice Row

Ducks and Ducklings and Grandmother's Choice are similar. Duck and Ducklings has pieced squares with a large triangle, and Grandmother's Choice has a square with a large triangle.

Both of my Grandmothers raised ducks and chickens. My sisters tell me I'm much like Grandma Knoechel, my paternal grandmother. We adored her! I can tell we were all excited about my Father's new truck!

On the maternal side was Mom Drushel. She lived close by in Harmony, Pennsylvania. We'd walk two miles just to visit and get a piece of her fresh baked bread!

Grandmother's Choice, *Page 135*

Ducks and Ducklings, *Page 134*

*Left to right -
Grandma
Knoechel,
Patty,
Eleanor,
Kathy*

Mom with her brother Clarence

36

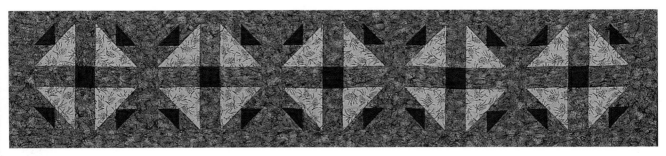

Cutting for Five Duck and Ducklings Blocks

For a simpler block minus Pieced Squares, sew Grandmother's Choice on page 43.

10½" Unfinished Size

Spring
Summer *Winter* *Fall*

Ground

Pieced Squares
  (3) 6" squares

Small Triangles
  (2) 2½" strips cut into
    (20) 2½" x 3¼" rectangles

Interior Lattice
  (3) 2½" strips cut into
    (20) 2½" x 4½" rectangles

Block Dividers
  (1) 2½" strip cut into
    (4) 2½" x 10½" pieces
  (2) 4½" x 10½" pieces

Row Divider
  (2) 2½" strips

Small Triangles

Pieced Squares
  (3) 6" squares

Center Squares
  (5) 2½" squares

Large Triangles

(2) 4½" strips cut into
  (10) 4½" x 5¼" rectangles

Making Twenty Pieced Squares

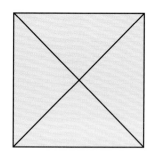

1. Place three 6" squares Ground right sides together to three 6" Pieced Squares. Place the lightest fabric on top, wrong side up. Press.

2. Draw two diagonal lines, corner to corner.

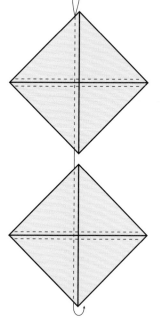

3. Continuously sew an accurate ¼" from one diagonal line. Turn the squares and sew ¼" on opposite side of diagonal line.

4. Clip squares apart.

5. Sew ¼" from both sides of second diagonal line. Clip squares apart.

6. Press to set seams.

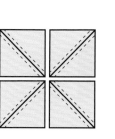

7. Place on gridded cutting mat. Using ruler and lines on mat, cut into 3" squares.

8. Cut on diagonal lines.

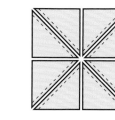

9. Place on pressing mat with Pieced Square fabric on top, open, and press against seam.

10. Square to 2½". There will be four extra Pieced Squares.

Making Twenty Corner Patches

1. Lay out (20) 2½" x 3¼" Ground rectangles with 20 Pieced Squares. Place Small Triangle next to Ground rectangle pointing downward.

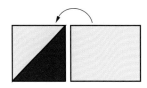

2. Flip rectangle right sides together to Pieced Square. Assembly-line sew a ¼" seam.

3. Press seam to Triangle.

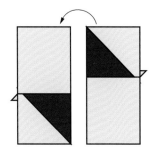

4. Lay out two pieces in the order shown here.

5. Make two stacks of ten pairs. Flip pieces right sides together, and assembly-line sew.

The seams are not supposed to match.

6. Clip the seam in the middle to the stitching.

7. Press, pushing the clipped seam to the rectangles.

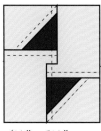

8. The patch should measure 4½" x 5¼". Sliver trim if necessary.

4½" x 5¼"

9. Turn patch wrong side up. Lay the diagonal line of the 6" x 12" ruler on a short side. Shift the ruler until the ruler's edge is at the point of the Pieced Square. **See lower circle.** The point of the ruler should be at the top edge of the patch. **See upper circle.**

10. **Draw a pencil line that will be your sewing line.**

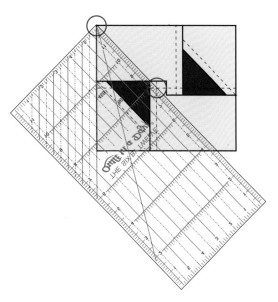

11. Turn the patch, and draw another sewing line across the point of the other Pieced Square. The distance between the parallel lines drawn on the diagonal is about ½", or two seam allowances.

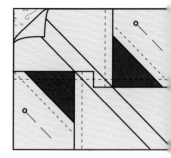
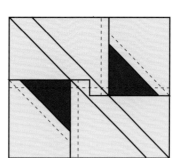

12. Layer patches right sides together with (10) 4½" x 5¼" Large Triangle rectangles.

13. Press and pin.

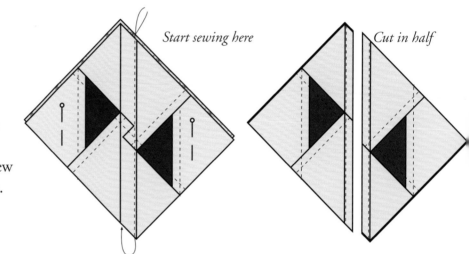

Start sewing here

Cut in half

14. Assembly-line sew on left side of the drawn lines. Turn and assembly-line sew on left side of second line.

15. Cut between the lines.

16. Set the seams with Large Triangle on top. Open, and press the seam to the Large Triangle.

17. Trim the tips.

18. The patch should measure 4½" square. Sliver trim if necessary.

Sewing Block Together

1. Lay out patches with 2½" x 4½" Interior Lattice pieces and 2½" Center Squares. Place five pieces in each stack.

2. Flip the middle vertical row right sides together to left vertical row.

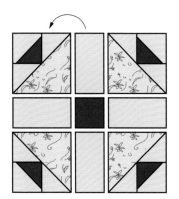

3. Assembly-line sew. Do not clip connecting threads.

4. Flip remaining row right sides together to middle row. Assembly-line sew. Clip between blocks, or every third piece.

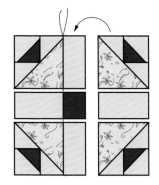

5. Sew outside rows to middle row, locking center seams by pushing seams away from Triangle and Center Square.

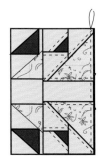

6. Press seams toward Interior Lattice.

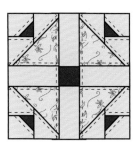

Sewing Row Together

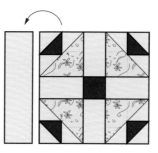

1. Stack four blocks with four 2½" x 10½" Block Dividers.

2. Flip blocks right sides together to Dividers. Assembly-line sew.

3. Set seams with strip on top, open and press toward strip.

4. Sew five blocks into one row.

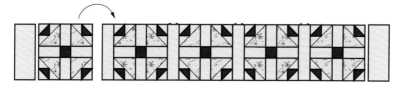

5. Sew remaining 4½" x 10½" strips to each end.

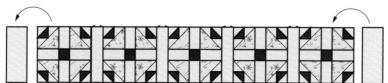

Adding Row Divider

1. Sew 2½" Ground strips into one long strip.

2. Pin and sew to bottom of row. Trim ends even.

3. Press seam away from blocks.

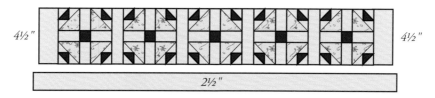

4½"   4½"

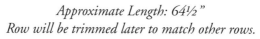

2½"

Approximate Length: 64½"
Row will be trimmed later to match other rows.

Grandmother's Choice Row

Make this row in place of the Duck and Ducklings Row.

Grandmother's Choice Row
has solid squares instead of
Pieced Squares in the corners.

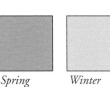

Spring
Summer   *Winter*   *Fall*

Ground

Small Triangles
> (2) 3¼" strips

Interior Lattice
> (3) 2½" strips cut into
>> (20) 2½" x 4½" rectangles

Block Dividers
> (1) 2½" strip cut into
>> (4) 2½" x 10½" pieces
> (2) 4½" x 10½" pieces

Row Divider
> (2) 2½" strips

Corner Squares
> (2) 2½" strips

Center Squares
> (5) 2½" squares

Large Triangles
> (2) 4½" strips cut into
>> (10) 4½" x 5¼" rectangles

Making Ten Corner Patches

This method yields two patches in one operation.

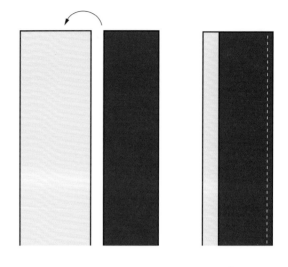

1. Sew two 2½" Corner Square strips right sides together to two 3¼" Ground strips.

2. Set seams with Corner Square on top, open, and press against seam.

3. Measure width of strips. They should measure 5¼".

This section should measure 5¼" wide. Adjust your seam if necessary.

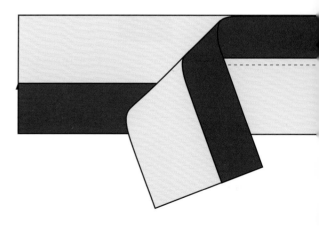

4. Layer first strip right side up on gridded cutting mat with Ground across top. Place second strip right sides together to it with Corner Square across top. **Seams do not match**. Line up strips with grid.

5. Square left end. Cut (10) 2½"
   pairs. Stack on spare ruler to carry
   to sewing area.

Cut (10) 2½ " pairs.

6. Assembly-line sew.

7. Clip seam in the middle to the stitching.

8. Press, pushing the clipped seam to
   the rectangles.

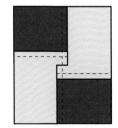

9. Follow directions for Ducks and Ducklings
   beginning on the bottom of page 39.

Stars of Friendship Row

Placemats,
Page 138

Tablerunner, *Page 139*

Tablerunner, *Page 138*

Left to right -
Kathy, Eleanor, Patty

Left to right -
Jackie, Eleanor, Linda

Have you ever thought of your friends as stars in your life? They are the people that brighten your day. When I was growing up, my sisters were my best friends, and they have remained bright spots in life. And there were friends like Jackie Creeks and Linda Geis that were as bright as the candles on my birthday cake. They were stars of friendship.

46

Cutting for Five Stars

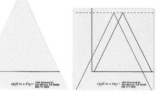

Triangle in a Square Rulers
Or Templates traced on Template Plastic

Patterns on page 14

*Spring
Summer* *Winter* *Fall*

Sky

Points
   (2) 4" strips

Corners
   (2) 3½" strips cut into
      (20) 3½" squares

Side and Corner Triangles
   (1) 14" strip cut into
      (2) 14" squares
   (2) 7½" squares

Ends of Row
   (2) 2" x 14" strips

Star Points

(2) 5" strips

Star Center Squares

(5) 3½" squares

Making Star Points

1. Layer the two 5" Star strips **wrong sides together. This step is essential for mirror image pieces.** With the 6" Square Up ruler, layer cut (**10**) **pairs** of 2½" x 5" rectangles for a total of 20.

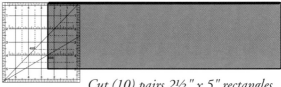
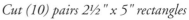

Cut (10) pairs 2½" x 5" rectangles

2. Layer cut on one diagonal. Sort these small triangles so they are right sides up.

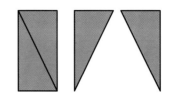

3. Layer 4" Sky strips right side up. Place Triangle on strip, **accurately lining up the narrow part** of the triangle with the strip. The bottom is not as critical.

Template: Trace 20 triangles on strip, turning template each time. Cut with ruler and rotary cutter.

Triangle in a Square ruler: Line up red line on Triangle ruler with edge of strip. Cut 20 Triangles with rotary cutter, turning ruler with each cut.

4. Lay out Sky Triangle with the base at the bottom. Position Star triangles on both sides. Make sure all fabrics are turned right side up.

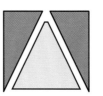

5. Set the right stack aside. Flip the Sky Triangle right sides together to the Star triangle.

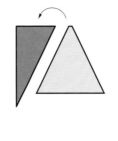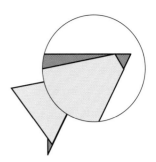

6. Position the triangles so the Star fabric extends beyond the Sky Triangle at the top, creating a tip at the flat top. Star triangle fabric also extends at the bottom.

7. Assembly-line sew with an accurate ¼" seam. Use stiletto to guide pieces. Check that seams are still ¼" at points.

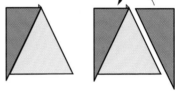

8. Place on pressing mat with Star triangles on top. Set seams, open, and press toward Star triangle.

9. Place the remaining Star triangle to the right of the Sky triangle.

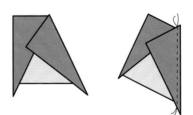

10. Flip right sides together, lining the top tip of both pieces together. Assembly-line sew.

11. Set seams with Star triangle on top, open, and press toward the triangle.

Squaring Up Triangle in a Square Patches

Patches are squared to 3½" with seam ¼" from top, and
⅛" from corners.

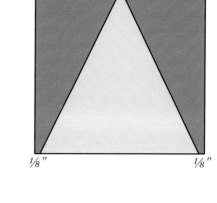

1. **Template:** Tape to underneath corner of 6" x 6" ruler.

2. Place ruler on patch. Line up red triangle lines with
   seams. Trim patch on right and top sides. Turn patch.
   Do not turn ruler. Line up red square lines with cut
   edges. Trim patch on remaining two sides to 3½"
   square.

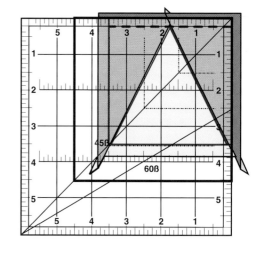

3. **Triangle in a Square Ruler:** Place square ruler on
   patch. Line up red triangle lines on ruler with
   seams. Trim patch on right side and top.

4. Turn patch. **Do not turn ruler.** Line up red square
   lines with cut edges. Trim patch on remaining two
   sides to 3½" square.

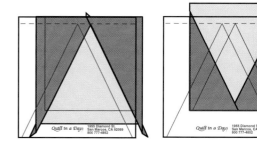

Sewing Block Together

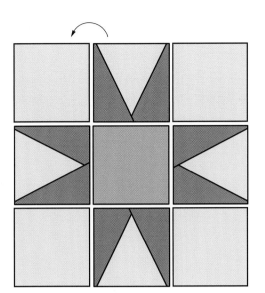

1. Lay out Star Points with 3½" Sky squares and 3½" Star Center squares. Place five pieces in each stack.

2. Flip middle vertical row to patches on left.

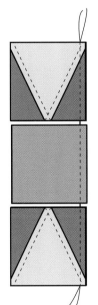
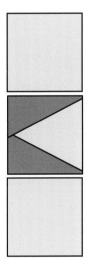

3. Matching outside edges, assembly-line sew.

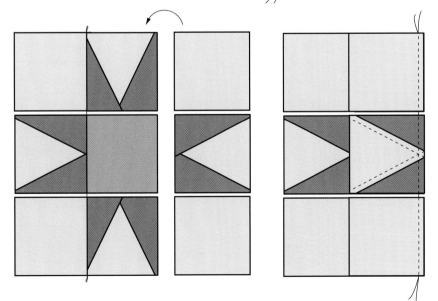

4. Flip right vertical row to middle row. Assembly-line sew.

5. Clip apart after every Star, or every third row.

6. Flip row on right to middle row. Press seams away from Star Points, and lock together.

7. Assembly-line sew. Clip Stars apart.

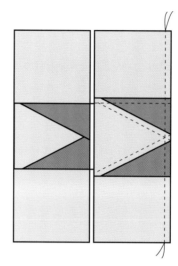

8. Flip middle row to last row, press seams away from Star points, lock, and assembly-line sew.

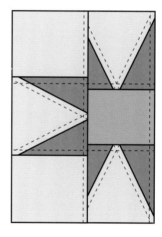

9. Clip Stars apart, and press seams toward center row.

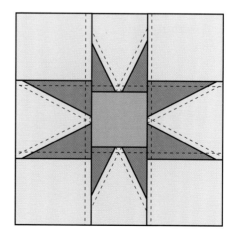

Adding Side Triangles

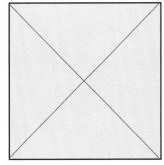
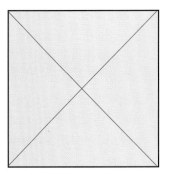

1. Cut (2) 14" Sky squares on both diagonals into triangles.

2. Stack five Sky triangles right side up beside five Star blocks.

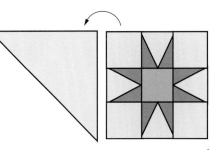

3. Flip Star block right sides together to triangle, matching top edges, and ⅜" tip extending at bottom. Pin together so bias on triangle does not stretch.

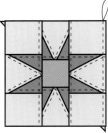

4. Assembly-line sew with triangle on bottom. Clip apart.

5. Set seams with triangle on top, open, and press toward triangle.

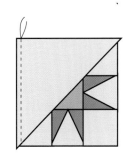

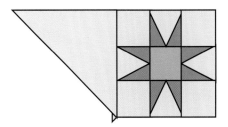

6. Count out **three Stars** with triangles attached. Stack three additional triangles beside them.

7. Flip Star block right sides together to triangle, matching top edges, and ⅜" tip extending at bottom. Pin and sew. Clip apart.

8. Set seams with triangle on top, open, and press toward triangle.

9. Straighten edges, lining up 6" x 24" ruler with sides of Star.

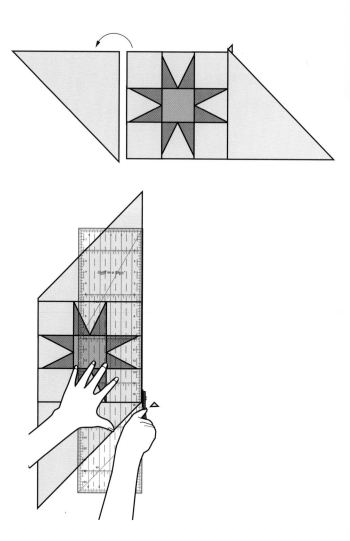

Adding Corner Triangles

1. Cut (2) 7½" Sky squares on one diagonal into triangles.

2. Stack two triangles beside two remaining Stars with triangles attached.

3. Flip triangle right sides together to Star, center, and pin. Sew with triangle on bottom.

4. Set seams, open, and press toward triangle. Straighten edges.

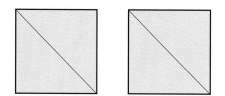

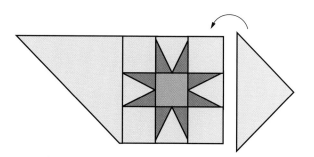

5. Stack remaining triangles beside Stars, flip right sides together, and pin. Sew with triangle on bottom.

6. Set seams, open, and press toward triangle.

7. Straighten edges.

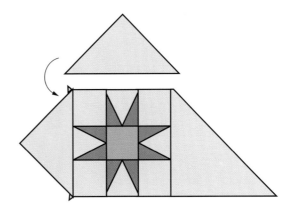

Finishing the Row

1. Lay out all pieces.

2. Sew together, matching seams. Tips of triangles extend on both ends. Press.

3. Measure against Four Patch Row. If Stars are shorter, add 2" x 14" strips to ends of row.

4. Straighten the edges, retaining a ¼" seam allowance around outside.

2" x 14"   *2" x 14"*

Approximate Finished Length: 66"
Row will be trimmed later to mach other rows.

Celebrating Angels Row

I know I have Angels on my shoulders. My sewing angel was my high school home economics teacher, Mrs. Gross. She took the mystery out of patterns and instructions, and helped me magically turn fabric into beautiful things. Thank heavens for Angels.

Guardian Angel Wallhanging, *Page 140*
Tooth Fairy Pillow, *Page 142*

Eleanor with Handsewn dress

PROFESSORATE PROVES PROFICIENT

Ruth Gross
Thiel College;
Geneva College, B.S.B.A.

Albert Bender

Cutting for Two Angels

Make the Angels holding a Banner, page 62, or a Garland, page 67.

15¾" x 64½" Unfinished Size

Spring Summer   *Winter*   *Fall*

Sky

(2) 15¾" strips cut into 15¾" x 34" pieces

Dresses and Sleeves

(1) 12" square

Dress Bottoms

(1) 3½" x 12"

Wings

(1) 11" square

Lace for Dresses

12" of lace 1" wide

Banner

(1) 9" x 22" rectangle

Hair

(1) 8" square

Letters

4½" x 22" rectangle

Halos

(1) 8" square

Fusible Interfacing

1 yard

Heads, Hands, Feet

(1) 8" square

Fusible Webbing

12" x 28" rectangle

Adding Lace to the Dresses

1. With seam slightly less than ¼", edgestitch 1" wide lace to 12" side of Dress Bottom.

2. With right sides together, sew Bottom to Dress.

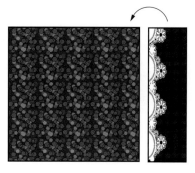

Tracing Patterns

1. Find Angel pattern in back of book.

2. Feel non-woven fusible interfacing. One side is smooth; the opposite side is textured with the fusing. Place interfacing on pattern sheet with smooth side up.

3. Trace patterns with fine point permanent marking pen. Keep patterns together that are to be made from the same fabric. Allow at least ½" space between pieces. Include lace lines on Dresses, and dashed lines.

4. Rough cut groups of patterns for same fabric. Do not cut out patterns on outside lines. These lines are sewing lines.

5. Place traced patterns with dotted, fusible side of interfacing against right side of appropriate fabric. Pin in center of pieces.

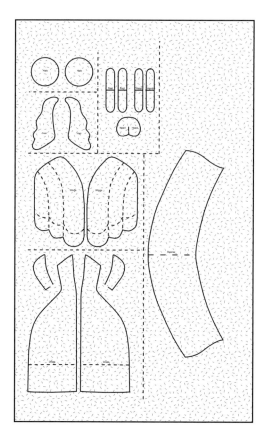

6. Line up the Lace Line on the interfacing with the Lace on the Dress. Pin in place.

Sewing the Pieces

1. Using an open toe **metal presser foot**, sew on the lines with setting 1.8 or 20 stitches per inch. Sew completely around the pieces, overlapping beginning and ending stitches.

2. With small 5" trimming scissors, trim ⅛" away from the lines.

3. Clip inside curves on Wings and Hair.

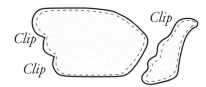

4. Cut Head, Hands, and Feet in half on dotted lines.

5. On remaining pieces, carefully clip a small slit in the center of the interfacing.

6. Cut a fat drinking straw in half. Insert into the slit. Push end of straw against the fabric. Stretch fabric over end of straw.

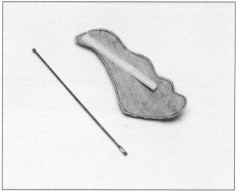

Ball point bodkin and drinking straw

7. Place the ball of the ball point bodkin on the fabric stretched over the straw end. Gently push fabric into straw with the bodkin. This technique begins to turn the piece. **Do not push piece through straw and out other end.**

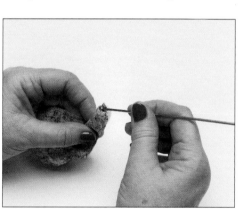

8. Remove the straw and bodkin. If necessary, insert straw and turn second half of applique with bodkin. Finish turning with fingers.

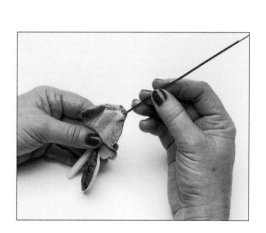

9. Push out edges by running bodkin around
   the inside of the piece.

10. Pull out points with stiletto or pin.

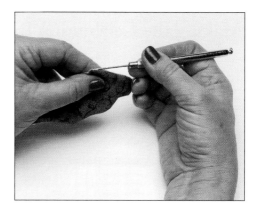

11. Smooth outside edges with a small wooden
    "pressing stick", or wooden iron. From
    right side, push fabric over interfacing edge.

12. Cut 100% cotton batting same size for
    Wings, Hair, Hands, Feet and Face. Stuff
    using hemostats.

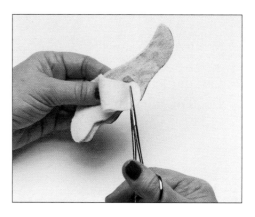

13. **Angel Wings:** Topstitch on lines.
    Optional: Topstitch lines when
    machine quilting.

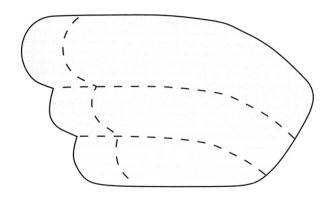

Making the Celebration Banner

1. Find letter patterns in back of book. Letters are mirror
   image because the process will reverse finished letters.

2. Cut paper backed webbing into
   4¼" strips. Center paper backed
   fusible webbing on letters with
   paper side up.

3. Trace letters.

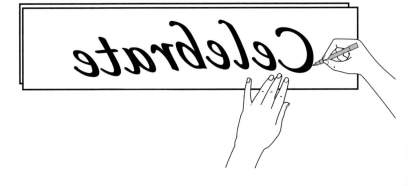

4. Place paper side up on wrong side of fabric. Press according
   to manufacturer's directions for your particular product.

5. Allow the fabric to cool.

6. Cut out letters on lines. For letters as *e*, *a*, and *b*, cut out
   small openings by slashing. Remove the paper backing.

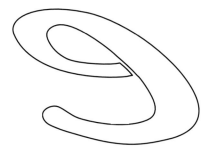

7. Place Banner on applique pressing cloth or brown paper bag to prevent fusible interfacing on back of Banner from sticking. Carefully space and arrange letters on Banner.

8. Fuse a few letters at a time. Follow manufacturer's directions. Peel off pressing cloth.

9. Depending on the product used, stitch letters in place, or leave unstitched.

Placing Pieces

1. Sew 15¾" x 34" Sky strips together. Press seam open.

2. Place Sky fabric on pressing mat. Center Banner on center seam. Drop down 2" from top edge. Measure Banner ends so they are equally spaced from top edge. Fuse Banner in place.

Angel Fusing Technique with Applique Pressing Cloth

1. Place pressing cloth on 16" Square Up Ruler. Place Angel placement sheet underneath ruler.

2. Assemble Angel pieces on pressing cloth.

3. Slide pressing cloth from ruler onto pressing mat or electronic press.

4. Fuse into one unit so Angel can be easily moved.

Angel Fusing Technique without Applique Pressing Cloth

1. Assemble Angel pieces on top of placement sheet. Pin pieces together.

2. Remove pins just before pressing.

Finishing

1. Slip Angels onto Sky fabric. Place with Hands touching Banner. Arrange both Angels with equal spacing from edges of Sky fabric.

2. Fuse Angels in place with a steam iron or electronic press.

Sewing Outside Edges

Using one of these hand or machine finishing methods, stitch around outside edges of Banner and Angels. If interfacing shows on edge of applique, roll it under with your stiletto.

Blind Hem or Applique Stitch

1. Set up your machine with invisible thread on the top and thread to match your Sky in the bobbin. Loosen your top tension. Use a small or #70 needle.

2. Set your stitch length at 2.0, or 15 stitches per inch. Set stitch width at 1.5.

3. Position the needle so the straight stitches line up with the edge on the Sky fabric, and the "bite" catches on the edge of the applique.

4. At the end of each piece, overlap the stitching, set your stitch width and length to "0", and stitch in place or lock stitch. Clip the threads.

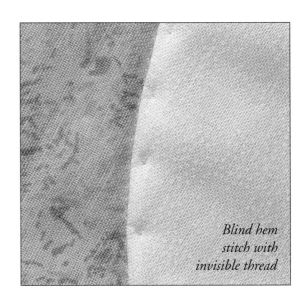

Blind hem stitch with invisible thread

Zig-zag Stitch with Invisible Thread

1. Use a narrow stitch width and length.

2. Catch both the applique and the Sky.

Zig-Zag Stitch

Blanket Stitch

1. Select a coordinating or contrasting color to outline each applique. Use regular or heavy thread in the top and regular matching thread in the bobbin. Use a stitch length of 3.0 and a width of 3.0.

2. Adjust the stitch so that the straight stitch lines up with the applique on the Sky fabric, and the "bite" is into the applique.

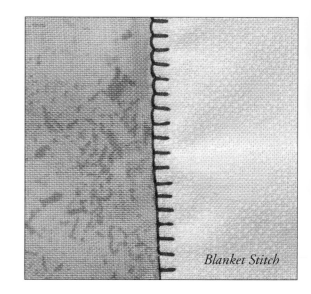

Blanket Stitch

Hand Applique

1. Thread #10 sharp or applique milliner's needle with 18" single strand of regular thread that matches the color of the applique. Pull thread through Thread Heaven or bees wax so it does not tangle.

2. Bring thread up through Sky fabric and catch just a couple of threads on the fold of the applique. Push needle down through Sky right above the spot where it came up.

3. Move the needle about ⅛" away, and come up through the Sky again. Pull stitches firmly but not too tightly. If interfacing shows on the edge of the applique, use tip of needle to tuck it under.

Sew a blind stitch that shows just a tiny spot of thread on the front and a slightly longer stitch on the back.

Garland Instructions

Garland and embellishments can be added before or after machine quilting. Pull Angel hands back and stitch Garland.

Garland

Garland

Cording

    1⅛ yds of ⅛" green cording

or

Machine Chain Stitch

    4 yds 4mm (⅛") green silk ribbon
    or 4 yds #3 green pearl cotton

Embellishments

Flowers

    (9) 1" ready made ribbon flowers
    (24) ½" ready made ribbon flowers

or

Folded Yo-Yos

    (5–9) 3" circles in assorted fabrics
    (21–31) ⅜" to ⅝" buttons in assorted colors
    3 yds 7 mm (¼") silk ribbon leaves for button flowers

Making the Garland Placement

1. **Town Square Quilt:** Position each Angel on Sky fabric 7½" from center, and 5" down from top edge.

2. **Wallhangings:** Position each Angel on Sky fabric 4" to 6" from center, and 5" down from top.

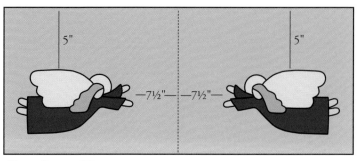

Town Square Placement

3. To draw the arc, make a pattern by folding an 11" x 17" piece of paper in half. Line up the paper's fold with the center of the Sky. Draw arc from center to Angel's hands, and cut out.

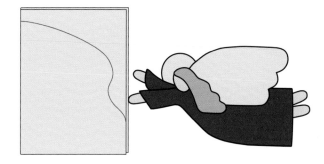

4. Open and position pattern between Angels hands.

Cord for Garland

1. Pull Angel hands back.

2. Arrange cord along arc.

3. Sew or glue in place with washable fabric glue.

Machine Chain Stitch for Garland

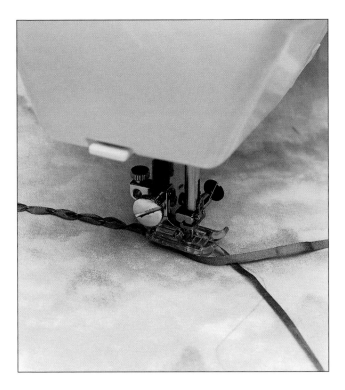

1. Pull Angel hands back.

2. With a pencil, trace arc onto Sky fabric.

3. Stabilize arc area by pinning paper underneath.

4. Match thread to 4mm silk ribbon or #3 pearl cotton.

5. Measure arc from center to end. Cut silk ribbon or pearl cotton twice that length plus a few inches.

6. Place center of ribbon on center of arc. Stitch back and forth to anchor.

7. Hold ends loosely. Criss-cross ribbon under presser foot.

8. Take three machine stitches. Stop with needle in the fabric.

9. Raise presser foot. Criss-cross ribbon in front of needle. Drop presser foot.

10. Stitch over ribbon, and take three machine stitches. Lift your presser foot each time you criss cross ends.

11. Continue to criss-cross and stitch until the arc is covered. Thread ribbon through large-eyed needle, and pull ends to back side. Knot.

12. Pull the paper away.

Folded Yo-Yos

1. Fold 3" circle in half, and crease center in both directions with steam iron.

2. Open, and fold outside edge to center. Press. Turn, and fold outside edge indicated by arrow to center. Press.

3. Turn, and fold outside edge indicated by arrow to center. Press.

4. Continue folding and pressing two more times.

5. Fold point to center.

6. Press, and sew small button to center.

Button Flowers

1. Cut 7mm (¼") green silk ribbon into 3" lengths, one for each flower.

2. Thread a hand sewing needle with matching green thread.

3. To make leaves in the shape of a figure 8, tuck one end under center, and stitch in place.

4. Tuck opposite end under center, and stitch again.

5. Sew button to center. If desired, tack down leaves after sewing in place.

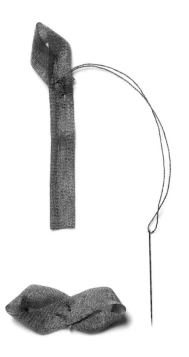

Adding Ready-made Flowers or Folded Yo-Yos to Garland

1. Place one large flower or yo-yo in the center. Work out to the ends, placing and balancing embellishments by alternating colors and sizes. Put smaller ones below the hands.

2. Glue or sew in place. Ready-made flowers can be removed when laundering quilt.

Silk ribbon roses were added after quilting.

Folded yo-yos and button flowers were added before quilting.

Trees on Main Street Row

Save the Trees, *Page 144*

Judy, Patty, Eleanor, Kathy

Father bordered the front of our home with pine trees. The trees were a perfect photo backdrop - they certainly accent our Easter dresses. It was my brother's job to keep the trees trimmed and the grass mowed. Father taught him young!

Bruce

Triangle and Flying Geese Trees

You can choose between patchwork trees or appliqued trees. If you want patchwork trees, make two Flying Geese Trees and three Triangle Trees. If you want appliqued trees, follow directions for seven trees on page 82.

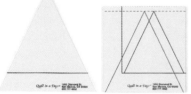

Triangle in a Square Rulers or Templates page 14.

Large Flying Geese Ruler with 2" x 4" markings or Templates, page 15.

Triangle Trees

Sky

Two Tall Triangle Trees
    (1) 5" strip

One Short Tree
    (2) 3" x 6"

Tree Top
    (1) 3½" x 5" rectangle

Five Trunks
    (1) 2⅛" strip cut into
        (2) 2⅛" x 21" pieces

Two Tall Trees
    (2) 4" x 12" pieces

One Short Tree
    (1) 5" x 6"

Five Trunks
(1) 1¼" x 21"

Flying Geese Trees

Sky

Trees
    (2) 7" squares

Tree Tops
    (1) 4½" x 6"
    (1) 4½" square

Trees
    (2) 5½" squares

Making Two Tall Triangle Trees

1. **Fold the 5" Sky fabric strip in half wrong sides together.** This step is essential for mirror image pieces. With 6" x 6" ruler, layer cut (4) 2½" x 5" pairs of rectangles, for a total of (8) rectangles.

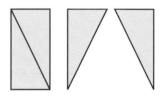

*(4) 2½" x 5" **pairs** of rectangles*

2. **Consistently** layer cut pairs of rectangles on one diagonal. Sort the triangles so they are right sides up.

3. Lay out (2) 4" x 12" Tree strips right side up. Line up red line on Triangle ruler with bottom edge of strip. **Cut eight Triangles.** Eliminate one.

Accurately lining up the top of the Triangle Ruler with the strip is most critical.

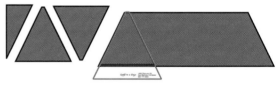

Cut eight triangles. Eliminate one.

4. Lay out the Tree Triangle with the base at the bottom. Position the smaller Sky Triangles on both sides of the Tree. Make sure all fabrics are turned right side up.

5. Set the right stack aside.

6. Flip the Tree right sides together over the Sky Triangle. The Sky fabric extends beyond the Tree to create a tip at the flat top of the Tree.

7. Sew. Set seams, open, and press toward smaller Sky Triangle.

8. Place the remaining Sky Triangle to the right of the Tree. Flip right sides together, lining the top tip of both pieces together.

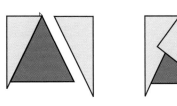

9. Sew and press toward the right triangle.

10. **Triangle in a Square Ruler or Template:** Line up red triangle lines with seams. Seams are ¼" from top edge, and ⅛" from corners. Trim patch on right and top edge.

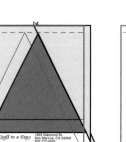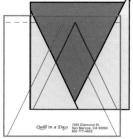

11. Lift ruler and turn patch. Line up red square lines with cut edges. Trim patch on remaining two sides to 3½" square.

Sewing Tall Triangle Trees Together

1. Make three stacks with two patches in each stack. Point your Triangles toward the left.

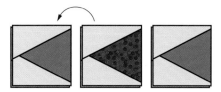

2. Assembly-line sew.

3. Add one more Triangle to the top of one Tree.

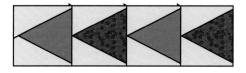

4. Add 3½" x 5" Sky to top of
   Tree with three Triangles.

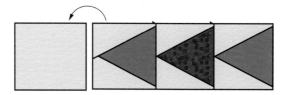

5. Press seams toward top of Tree.

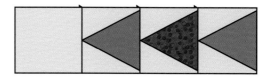

Making One Short Tree

1. Place (2) 3" x 6" Sky rectangles wrong side
   together. Layer cut on one diagonal.

2. Turn all Triangles right side up. Eliminate
   the two extra triangles.

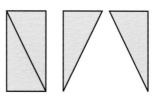

3. Lay out the 6" x 5" Tree fabric. Carefully line
   up top of Triangle Ruler with top of strip.
   Cut 5" Triangle.

4. Position Sky triangles on both sides of Tree
   Triangle.

5. Sew left Sky Triangle, set seam, open and
   press toward Sky.

6. Sew right Sky Triangle, set seam, open, and
   press toward Sky.

7. Trim patch on all four sides to 4½" square.

Making Two Flying Geese Trees

1. Place the 5½" Tree squares right sides together and centered on the 7" Sky squares. Press.

2. With the 6" x 12" ruler, draw a diagonal line across the squares. Pin.

3. Sew exactly ¼" from both sides of drawn line. Press to set seam.

4. Cut on drawn line.

5. Place on pressing mat with larger triangle on top. Set seams, open, and press seams to **larger triangle**. Size of triangle is important, not color of triangle, for proper pressing.

6. Place squares right sides together so that opposite fabrics touch.

7. Match up the outside edges. Notice that there is a gap between the seams. **The seams do not lock.**

8. Draw a diagonal line across the seams. Pin.

9. Sew ¼" from both sides of drawn line. Press to set seam.

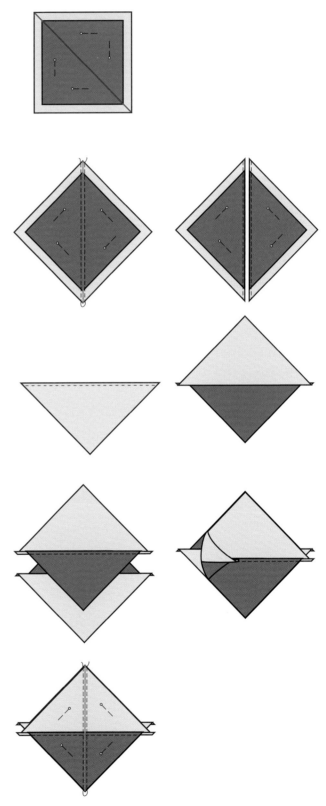

10. Cut on the drawn line.

11. Clip the seam allowance to the vertical seam midway between the horizontal seams. This allows the seam allowance to be pressed to the fabric of the original larger square.

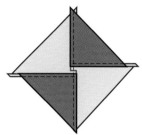

12. Press each half open, pushing the clipped seam allowance to the fabric of the larger square.

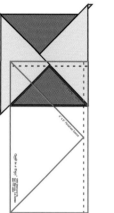

13. Place the Geese on a small cutting mat so you can rotate the mat as you cut.

14. Select the Flying Geese ruler with the 2" x 4" Finished Geese marking. Place the ruler in a vertical position. Line up the ruler's red triangle lines on the 45° sewn lines. Line up the red dotted line with the peak of the triangle for the ¼" seam allowance.

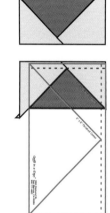

15. Cut the block in half to separate the two patches. Trim off excess fabric, turning the mat as you cut. Hold the ruler securely on your fabric so it will not shift while you are cutting.

16. Lift the ruler. Turn the patch around. Trim excess fabric off the bottom of the Geese.

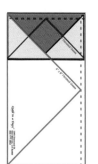

Sewing Geese Trees Together

1. Make two stacks with four Geese in each stack. Point your Geese toward the left.

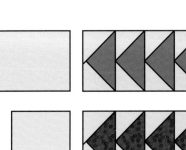

2. Assembly-line sew into two sets of four Geese.

3. Sew 4½" x 6" Sky to top of one Tree and 4½" square Sky to top of second Tree.

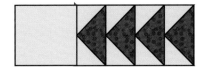

4. Press seams toward top of Tree.

Making Tree Trunks

1. Sew 2⅛" x 21" Sky strips to both sides of 1¼" x 21" Trunk strip.

2. Press seams toward Trunk. Width of Trunks should be 4½". If necessary, make an adjustment in your seam allowance.

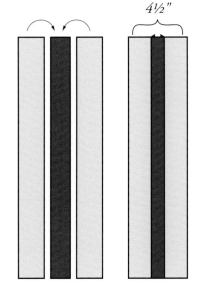

Finishing Trees

1. Cut (2) 5" pieces, (2) 3½" pieces, and (1) 1½" piece.

2. Center Trunks on bottom of Trees, so Trees are all approximately the same length. Trunks should match width of Geese Trees. Triangle Trunks will be wider.

3. Assembly-line sew.

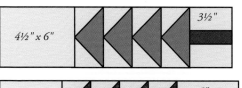

4. Trim Triangle Trunks to match width of Triangles.

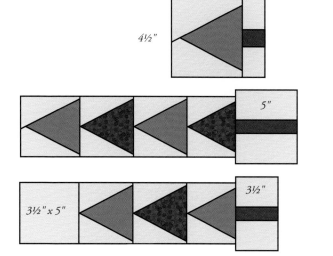

Trim sides of trunks.

5. Trim Tall Trees to 16" in length, by trimming off Trunk or Sky. Set aside until buildings are completed.

6. Set Short Tree aside until Cottage, page 91.

Making Applique Trees

Trees
(3) 9" x 12" pieces

1. Following applique directions on pages 58 to 61, trace two large, three medium, and two small Trees on the smooth side of the non-woven fusible interfacing.

2. Place fusible side of interfacing against right side of Tree fabric. Pin.

3. Sew, trim, turn, and stuff.

4. Set aside until buildings are completed.

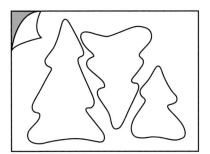

Applique Tree Patterns

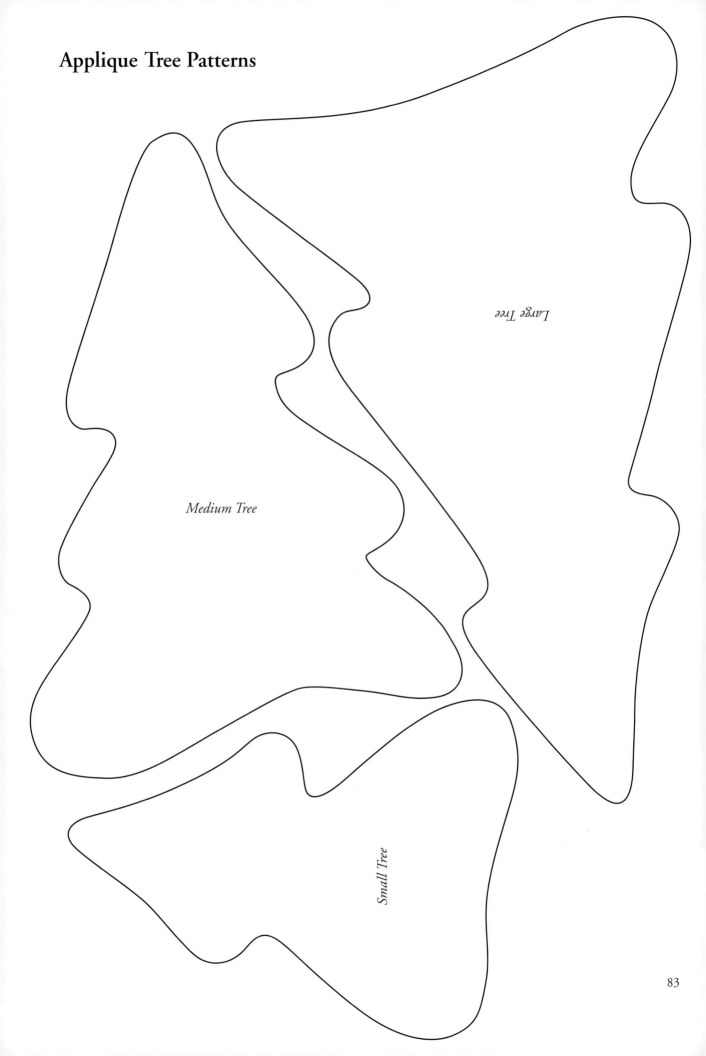

Large Tree

Medium Tree

Small Tree

Main Street Row – Church

What fond memories I have of growing up within the church family. Playing the piano, parts in Christmas pageants, and singing in the choir were all a scary part of maturing and gaining confidence. I remember Mother and Daughter Banquets, and Luther League with boy/girl games. One of those Sunday nights was the first time I kissed a boy! And look where it lead me!

Angels on High, *Page 148*

Eleanor and Bill on their wedding day

Teresa's Church, *Page 154*

Cutting for One Church Block

All yardage is given width x height. This is important if you are using a directional fabric.

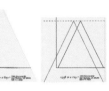

Triangle in a Square Rulers
Or Templates traced on Template Plastic
Patterns on page 14

16" Unfinished Size

Spring Summer   *Winter*   *Fall*

Sky

(1) 3" strip cut into
    (2) 3" x 16½"
    (2) 2½" squares
(2) 4½" x 5½"

Church

(2) 4½" x 7½"
(1) 4½" x 2½"
(2) 1½" x 5½"
(1) 6" x 5"
(1) 4½" x 3½"

Roof

(1) 4½" x 2½"
(2) 4½" squares
(2) 3" x 6"

Door

(1) 2½" x 5½"

Windows

(3) 3" x 4"

Cross

(1) 2½" x 3½"

Fusible Web

(1) 2" x 3"

Fusible Interfacing

(1) 4½" x 10"

85

Making the Door

1. Lay out one 1½" x 5½" Church fabric on each side of the 2½" x 5½" Door fabric.

2. Sew and press seams toward Church.

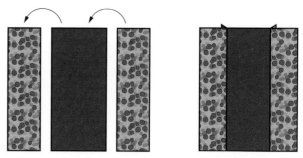

This section should measure 4½" x 5½".
Adjust your seam if necessary.

3. Sew the 4½" x 2½" Church piece to the top of the Door section.

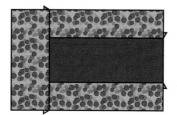

4. Press seams toward Church fabric.

Making the Middle Roof Section

1. Layer the two 3" x 6" Roof pieces **wrong sides** together. Layer cut on one diagonal.

2. Turn all Triangles right side up. Sort into two mirror image Triangles. Eliminate the extra two.

3. Lay out the 6" x 5" Church fabric. Carefully line up top of triangle with top of strip. **Template:** Trace and cut out one 5" triangle.

   Triangle in a Square Ruler: Cut out one 5" Triangle.

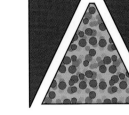

4. Position Roof Triangles on both sides of Church Triangle.

5. Sew left Roof Triangle, set the seam, open, and press toward Roof.

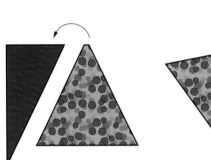

6. Sew right Roof Triangle, set seam, open, and press toward Roof.

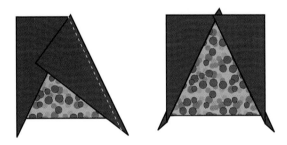

7. Place patch on small cutting mat.

8. Place Triangle in a Square Ruler on patch. Line up turquoise triangle lines on seam.

9. Trim on all four sides to 4½" square. Rotate cutting mat as you trim, leaving patch and ruler in place.

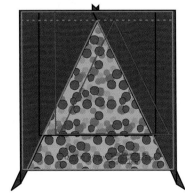

Making the Top Roof Section

1. On the wrong sides of two 2½" Sky squares, draw a diagonal line.

2. Place one Sky square right sides together to the 4½" x 2½" Roof piece. Sew on the drawn line. Trim ¼" from line.

3. Press seam toward the Sky.

4. Sew remaining 2½" Sky square to the Roof. Trim ¼" from line.

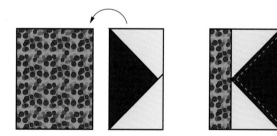

5. Press seam toward the Sky.

6. Sew Top Roof to the 4½" x 3½" Church piece.

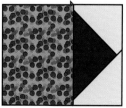

7. Press seam toward Church fabric.

Completing the Church

1. Lay out pieces for block.

2. Flip middle vertical row to left and assembly-line sew.

3. Flip vertical row on right to middle row and assembly-line sew. Do not clip connecting threads.

4. Sew remaining rows, pushing seams toward the Middle Roof triangle and away from the Door and Top Roof.

5. Press seams away from Middle Roof sections

6. Sew one 3" x 16½" Sky strip to both sides of the Church, starting at the top and sewing down. Press seams toward the Sky.

7. Center a 16" Square Up ruler on the block. Match top edge of ruler to top edge of block. Place ruler lines parallel with seams. Trim on sides and bottom to 16" square.

8. Applique two large Windows and Cross or two large and one small Window.
   Optional: Place Cross on top of Church after quilt is sewn together. See page 106.

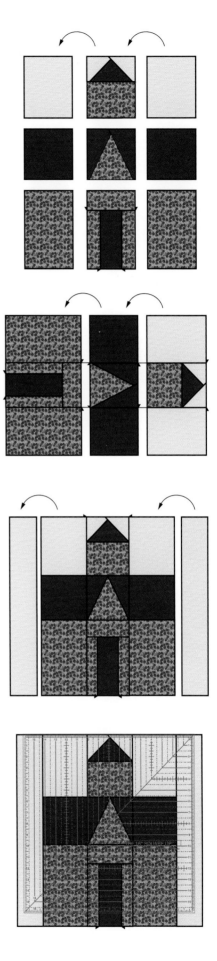

89

Main Street Row – Cottage

Our first home was a little cottage just outside of town. Aunt Donna and Grace, Uncle Larry, and Cissie Bintrim came to my second birthday party in that little cottage. It looks like Kathy enjoyed the party too! Memories of the meadow beside the cottage, beautiful with blue bells in the spring, and meandering brook linger still.

Quilt Show Wallhanging, *Page 152*

Mother

Mother and Eleanor

Cottage in the Country, *Page 156*

*Top Row -
Kathy, Eleanor, Grace
Bottom Row -
Larry, Cissie, Donna*

Cutting for One Cottage Block

All yardage is given width x height. This is important if you are using a directional fabric. Use the 6" x 10½" Sky area to the right for appliqued trees, people, or flowers, or fill the area with the Short Triangle Tree, page 77.

16" Unfinished Size

Spring
Summer   Winter   Fall

Sky

(2) 4½" squares
(1) 3" x 10½"
(1) 16½" x 6½"

Applique Area
    (1) 6" x 10½"
or
Short Tree Area
    (1) 2" x 5½"
    (1) 6" x 5½"

Cottage

(1) 2½" strip for non-directional only cut into
    (1) 8½" x 2½"
    (2) 1½" x 2½"
    (1) 2½" x 4½"
    (1) 4½" x 2½"

Roof

(1) 8½" x 4½"

 ## Chimney

(1) 6" square

Door

(1) 2½" x 4½"

 ## Smoke

(1) 6" square

Window

(1) 2½" square

Making the Cottage

1. Sew the (2) 1½" x 2½" Cottage pieces on each side of 2½" square Window piece.

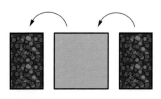

2. Press seams toward Cottage fabric.

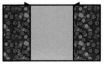

This piece should be 2½" x 4½". If yours is not, make an adjustment in your ¼" seam.

3. Sew Window section to 4½" x 2½" Cottage fabric.

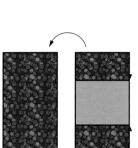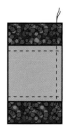

4. Press seam toward Cottage.

5. Sew 2½" x 4½" Cottage piece to 2½" x 4½" Door.

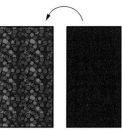

6. Press seam toward Door.

7. Sew Window section to Door section.

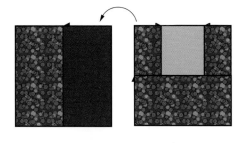

8. Press seams toward Door.

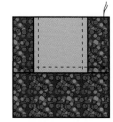

9. Sew Door/Window section to top of 8½" x 2½" Cottage piece.

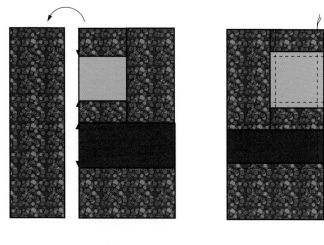

10. Press seam toward Cottage piece.

11. Sliver trim sides of Cottage to straighten.

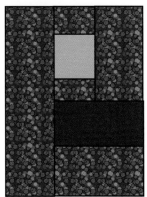

12. On the wrong side of the (2) 4½" Sky
    squares, draw a diagonal line.

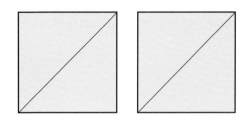

13. Place one 4½" Sky square right sides
    together to the 8½" x 4½" Roof. Sew on
    the drawn line. Trim ¼" from line.

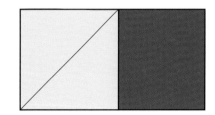

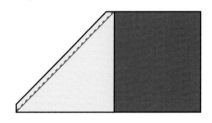

14. Press seam toward Sky.

15. Place remaining 4½" Sky square on Roof. Sew on line

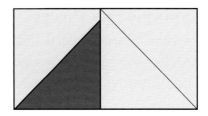

16. Trim ¼" from line. Press seam toward Sky.

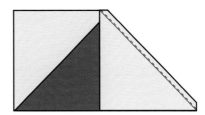

17. Add Roof to top of Cottage. Press seam toward Cottage.

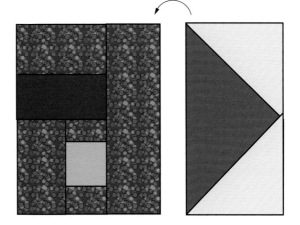

Adding the Applique Sky Pieces

1. Lay out the 3" x 10½" Sky on the left side of Cottage and the 6" x 10½" Sky to the right side of the Cottage. Starting from the top, sew together.

2. Press seams toward Sky.

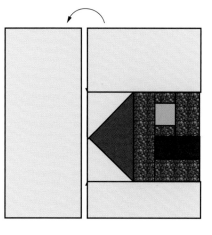

3. Sew Cottage to 16½" x 6½" Sky piece. Press seam toward Sky.

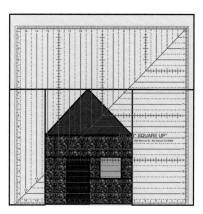

4. Center 16" Square Up ruler on block. Match bottom edge of ruler to bottom edge of Cottage. Place ruler lines parallel with seams. Square to 16".

5. Applique Chimney and Smoke found on page 106.

6. Applique people or flowers from printed fabrics. See Fussy Cuts on page 105.

Adding the Short Tree

Instructions for Short Tree are on page 77.

1. Sew the 2" x 5½" Sky strip to the left side of Short Tree. Press seam toward strip.

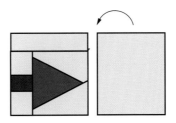

2. Sew 6" x 5½" Sky rectangle to top of Short Tree. Press seam toward rectangle.

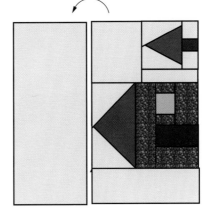

3. Starting from the bottom, sew Tree to right side of Cottage. Straighten top edge.

4. Sew the 3" x 10½" Sky strip to the left side of the Cottage.

5. Sew Cottage to 16½" x 6½" Sky piece. Press seam toward Sky.

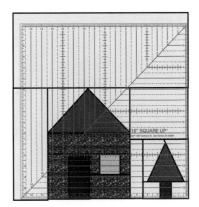

6. Place 16" Square Up ruler on block. Match bottom edge of ruler to bottom edge of Cottage. Match right side of ruler ¼" from edge of Tree. Square to 16".

7. Applique Chimney and Smoke are found on page 106.

Main Street Row – Schoolhouse

Amber's Schoolhouse, *Page 160*

My elementary school, Main Street School, was walking distance. My mother often sent me off with a fresh picked bouquet for Mrs. Gibson, the school crossing guard, and my teachers. I was shy then, and always followed the Golden rules! Zelienople High School was just a bit farther, but close enough to walk home for lunch. I was good at basketball . . . a guard, no less!

Top – Zelienople High School
Right – Main Street School

Cutting for One School Block

All yardage is given width x height. This is important if you are using a directional fabric.

  ## Sky

(2) 5½" squares
(2) 3½" squares
(2) 2½" squares
(1) 3" x 16½" strip

School

(2) 14½" x 1½"
(6) 1½" x 2½"
(3) 2½" squares
(2) 5½" x 2½"
(1) 4½" x 3½"

Windows

(6) 2½" squares

Door

(1) 4½" square

Roof

(1) 4½" x 2½"
(1) 14½" x 3½"

 ## Bell

(1) 3" square

Spring Summer   *Winter*   *Fall*

Making Door and Windows

1. Fold 4½" square Door in half. Finger press. Sew a decorative stitch such as a triple stitch on the fold to make the fabric look like two doors.

2. Assembly-line sew two 1½" x 2½" School pieces, two 2½" square Windows and two 2½" square School pieces.

3. Press seams toward School fabric.

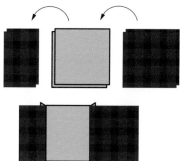

4. Sew one 5½" x 2½" School piece to the left side of the Window unit and one 5½" x 2½" School piece to the right of the Window unit.

5. Press seams toward School fabric.

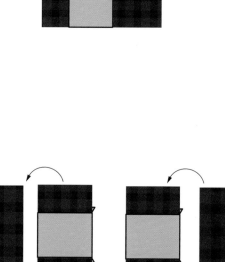

6. Turn pieces so the Windows are on the top. Sew one Window section to each side of the Door.

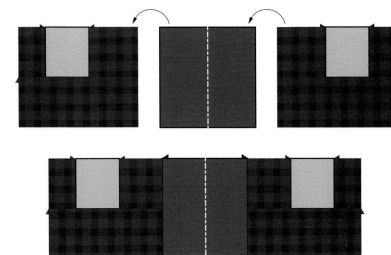

7. Press seams toward Door.

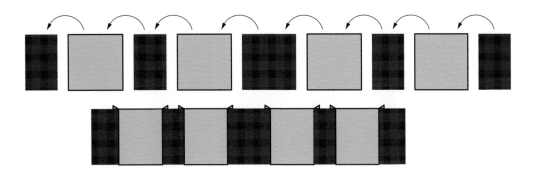

8. Lay out four 1½" x 2½" and one 2½" square School pieces with the remaining four 2½" square Windows. Sew and press the seams towards the school fabric.

9. Sew the School together using the two 14½" x 1½" School pieces. Press seams toward long strips. If necessary, sliver trim and square sides.

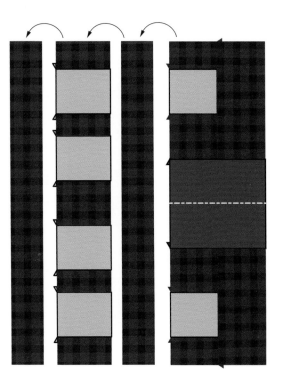

Middle Roof Section

1. Measure width of School. It should be 14½". Place the 14½" x 3½" Roof against the School to see if they are the same width. Trim Roof if necessary.

2. On the wrong sides of two 3½" Sky squares, draw a diagonal line.

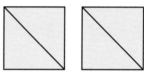

3. With right sides together, place a square on each end of the 14½" x 3½" Roof.

4. Sew on the drawn line. Trim excess ¼" from line.

5. Press seams toward the Sky. Sliver trim to straighten.

Top Roof Section

1. On the wrong sides of two 2½" Sky squares, draw a diagonal line.

2. With right sides together, place one square on one end of the 4½" x 2½" Roof. Sew on the drawn line.

3. Trim excess ¼" from line.

4. Press seam toward the Sky.

5. Sew remaining Sky square to the Roof. Trim excess.

6. Press seam toward the Sky.

7. Sew the Top Roof to the 4½" x 3½" School piece.

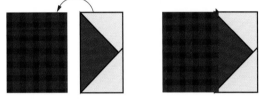

8. Press seam toward the School.

9. Sew one 5½" square Sky piece to each side of the top Roof.

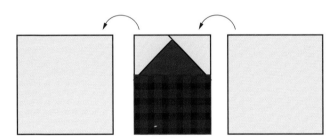

10. Press seams toward the Sky.

Completing the School Block

1. Sew the Top Roof, Middle Roof and School together. Press seams away from the Middle Roof.

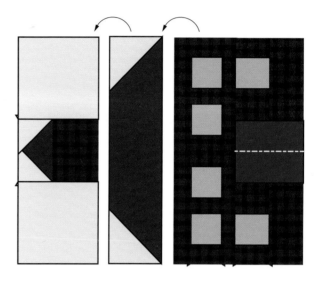

2. Place the 3" x 16½" Sky strip to the left side of the School, match at the top end and sew down. Press seams toward the Sky.

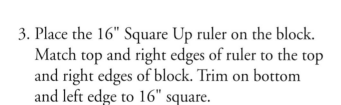

3. Place the 16" Square Up ruler on the block. Match top and right edges of ruler to the top and right edges of block. Trim on bottom and left edge to 16" square.

4. Applique the Bell, found on page 106.

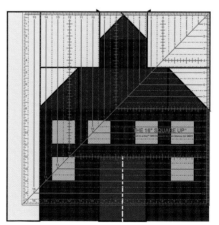

Applique Pieces for Main Street

Fussy Cuts from Printed Fabric

1. Select "fussy cut" from printed fabric, and rough cut.

2. On wrong side, trace ¹⁄₁₆" away from outline with permanent marking pen.

3. Place right side of "fussy cut" against dotted fusible side of interfacing.

4. Sew on the line with 20 stitches per inch.

5. Trim and turn right side out.

6. Fuse in position, and stitch around outside edge.

Applique Pieces for Main Street

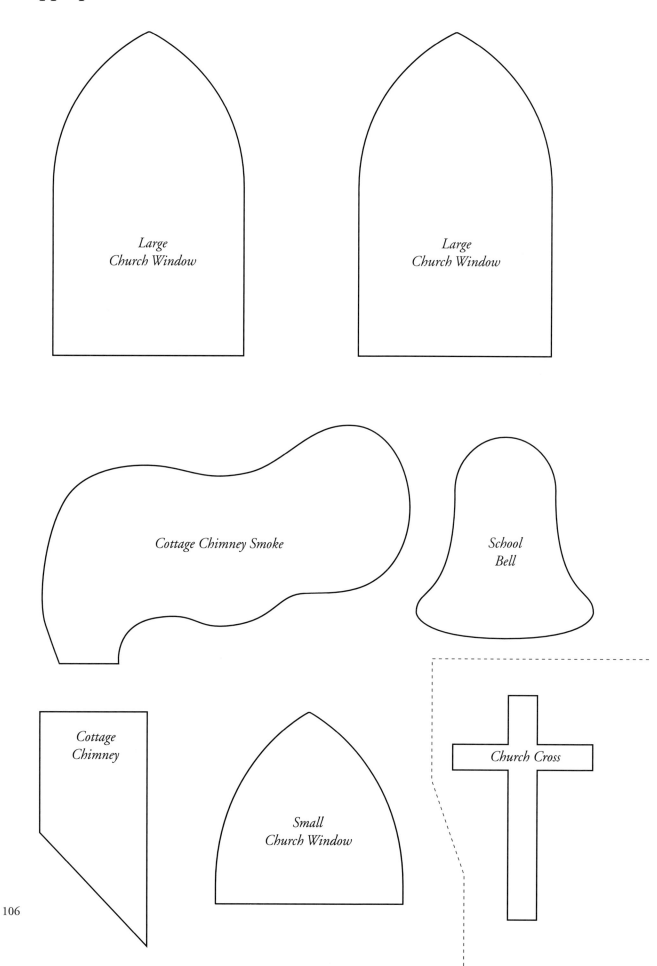

Large
Church Window

Large
Church Window

Cottage Chimney Smoke

School
Bell

Cottage
Chimney

Small
Church Window

Church Cross

Applique with Non-Woven Fusible Interfacing

Use this technique for the Church Windows, School Bell, Cottage Chimney and Chimney Smoke. See pages 58 – 61 for more information.

1. Trace patterns on smooth side of 8½" x 11" light to medium weight non-woven fusible interfacing. Rough cut around patterns. Place traced patterns with dotted, fusible side of interfacing against right side of appropriate fabric. Pin in place.

2. Sew on the lines with 20 stitches per inch, overlapping beginning and ending stitches. Trim ⅛" away from the lines. Clip a small slit in the center of the interfacing.

3. Turn right sides out with drinking straw and ballpoint bodkin.

4. Smooth outside edges with a small wooden "pressing stick." Cut cotton batting same size as applique and stuff using hemostats.

5. Place pieces on appropriate buildings and fuse in place with steam iron. Stitch around outside edges with blanket stitch and colored thread, or blind hem stitch and invisible thread.

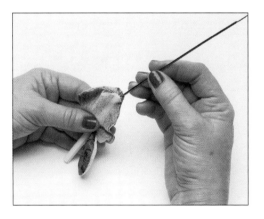

Applique with Paper Backed Fusible Web

Use this technique for the Church Cross in place of the Small Church Window.

1. Center 2" x 3" paper backed fusible webbing on Cross with paper side up. Trace on smooth side.

2. Place paper side up on wrong side of fabric. Press according to manufacturer's directions. Cool, and cut out on lines. Position and fuse Cross on Church.

3. Depending on product used, stitch in place, or leave unstitched.

Sewing Main Street Row Together
Patchwork Trees

 Sky
End Spacers
(2) 2½" x 16"

 Ground
Row Divider
(2) 3" strips

1. Lay out the three buildings with the trees. Make certain all buildings are squared to 16" and the Trees are 16" in height.

2. Pin and sew together. Press seams away from Trees.

3. Sew 2½" x 16" End Spacers to ends of row.

4. Sew 3" Ground strips into one long strip.

5. Pin and sew to bottom of Main Street.

6. Trim ends even. Press seam toward Ground.

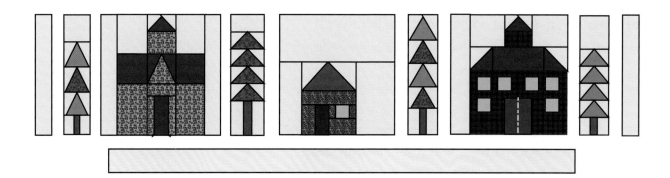

Applique Trees

Sky
(2) 6½" x 16"
(1) 4½" x 16"
(1) 3½" x 16"

Ground
Row Divider
(2) 3" strips

1. Lay out the three buildings. Make certain all buildings are squared to 16". Place Sky spacers between buildings.

2. Pin and sew together. Press seams toward Spacers.

3. Sew 3" Ground strips into one long strip.

4. Pin and sew to bottom of Main Street.

5. Trim ends even. Press seam toward Ground.

6. Position Trees in Spacers between the buildings.

7. Fuse in place. Sew around the outside edges.

Sewing the Top Together

1. Press each row from wrong side and right side.

2. Carefully mark center of each row with pins or disappearing marker on both top and bottom edges. Row lengths will differ.

3. Lay out Four Patch Row. Compare each row to Four Patch Row. Row lengths will differ, but make sure no rows are shorter than the Four Patch Row. If necessary, change width of spacers at ends of any shorter rows.

4. Trim all Rows to match Four Patch Row.

5. Place Four Patch Row right sides together to Stars Row.

6. Starting at center, match marks, and pin together from center out without stretching. Sew two rows together.

7. Match centers, pin, and sew Angels to bottom of Four Patch.

8. Match centers, pin, and sew Edna's Pinwheel to Main Street.

9. Match centers, pin, and sew Maple Leaves to Ducks and Ducklings.

10. Match centers, pin, and sew Maple Leaves to Edna's Pinwheel.

11. Match centers, pin, and sew top half to bottom half.

12. If necessary, straighten outside edges.

13. Press from wrong side.

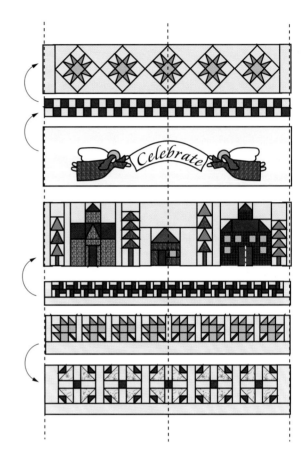

Finishing

Split Rail Border

6½" Unfinished Size

Cutting for Forty-eight Split Rail Blocks and Borders

First Dark

Rails
(8) 2" strips

First Border
(8) 2½" strips
(8) 2½" x 6½" rectangles

Corner Squares
(4) 6½" squares

Medium

Rails
(16) 2" strips

Second Dark

Rails
(8) 2" strips

Second Border
(9) 2½" strips

Sewing First Border

1. Square off selvage edges on (8) 2½" First Dark strips, and sew together into four long strips.

2. Measure long sides of quilt. Cut two pieces 2" longer.

3. With 1" extending on each end, pin and sew to sides of quilt.

4. Set seams, open, and press toward Border. Square ends.

5. Measure width of quilt from outside edge to the other, including Borders just added. Cut two pieces 2" longer.

6. With 1" extending on each end, pin and sew to quilt.

7. Set seams, open, and press toward Border. Square ends.

Making Forty-eight Split Rail Blocks

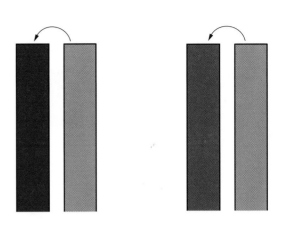

1. Sew (8) 2" First Dark and (8) 2" Medium strips right sides together. Use an accurate ¼" seam.

2. Sew (8) 2" Second Dark and (8) 2" Medium strips right sides together.

3. Set seams with darkest strip on top, open, and press against seam.

4. Measure width of strips. They should measure 3½".

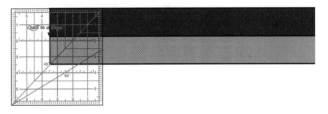

5. Layer strips right sides up on gridded cutting mat. Square left end.

6. Cut (96) 3½" pieces from each set of strips.

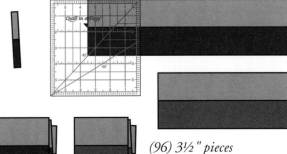

(96) 3½" pieces from each set

7. Divide into four stacks with 48 in each. Turn pieces in this order:

8. Flip top pieces right sides together to pieces on left.

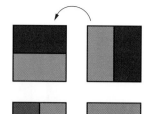

11. Clip apart every other pair. Open.

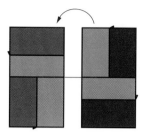

9. Matching outside edges, assembly-line sew. Use stiletto to pull outside edges together and hold seams flat.

10. Repeat with all pieces.

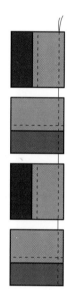

12. Flip right sides together, pushing top center seam down, and underneath center seam up.

13. Assembly-line sew, holding seams flat with stiletto.

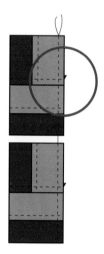

14. Divide into two piles of twenty-four blocks with First Dark on right and Second Dark on left.

15. Press seams in right stack toward First Dark. Press seams in left stack toward Second Dark. Set four blocks aside, two from each stack.

16. Turn left stack, so center seam goes down.

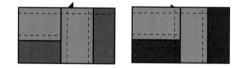

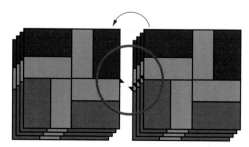

22 blocks in each stack

17. Flip top block right sides together to block on left, lock center seams, and match outside edges. Assembly-line sew into pairs.

Mary Hawkins made her Split Rail Border in patriotic red, white, and blue fabrics. Completing Mary's beautiful quilt is the flag waving in the warm summer breeze, children playing in the yard, and bright red birds flying over head.

Mary Hawkins

80" x 90"

Sewing Top and Bottom Split Rail Borders Together

1. Count out two stacks of five pairs each.

2. Sew together two rows of five pairs each, locking center seams.

3. Add one single block to end of each row, for a total of eleven blocks in two rows.

4. Sew 2½" x 6½" First Dark rectangles to ends of both rows.

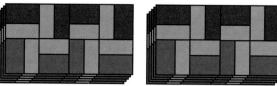

Five pairs for Top   *Five pairs for Bottom*

Sewing Side Split Rail Borders Together

1. Count out two stacks of six pairs each.

2. Sew together two rows of six pairs each, alternating and locking center seams.

3. Add one single block to end of each row, for a total of thirteen blocks in two rows.

4. Sew 2½" x 6½" First Dark rectangles to ends of both rows.

Six pairs for one side   *Six pairs for other side*

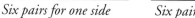

Trimming Split Rail Borders

1. Measure all four sides of quilt top. Find an average measurement for length and width.

2. Center Side borders against length of quilt top. Trim First Dark rectangles equally to match quilt length.

3. Center Top and Bottom borders against width of quilt top. Trim First Dark rectangles equally to match quilt width.

4. Pin and sew Side Split Rail Borders to sides of quilt.

5. Set seams, open, and press seams to First Border.

6. Sew First Dark 6½" Corner Squares to ends of Top and Bottom Split Rail Borders. Press seams to Corner Square.

7. Pin and sew Top and Bottom Split Rail Borders to quilt. Press seams to First Border.

Sewing Second Dark Border

1. Repeat same steps as in First Border.

2. Press top on wrong side and then on the right side.

Check the Fit

Lay the quilt top on your bed. Measure to find how much border you need to get the fit you want. Keep in mind, the quilt will "shrink" approximately 2" in length and width after completion of machine quilting.

Adding Fourth Borders

1. Square off the selvage edges, and sew 6" strips together lengthwise.

2. Measure the long sides of the quilt.

3. Cut two pieces the same length from the border fabric.

4. Pin the borders to the long sides.

5. Stitch from end to end. Fold them out flat.

6. Measure the top and bottom of the quilt from one outside edge to the other, including the borders just added.

7. Cut two borders that measurement.

8. Pin the borders to the top and bottom.

9. Stitch. Fold them out flat.

10. Press top.

Teresa Varnes   *90" x 100"*

Layering the Quilt

1. Spread the backing out on a large table or floor area with the right side down. Clamp the fabric to the edge of the table with quilt clips or tape it to the floor. Do not stretch the backing.

2. Layer the batting on top of the backing, and pat flat.

3. With the quilt top right side up, center on the backing. Smooth until all layers are flat. Clamp or tape outside edges.

4. Safety pin the layers together every three to five inches. Use a pinning tool to assist the process. Pin next to your quilting lines.

Machine Quilting Your Top

The ideal machine quilting area is a sewing machine bed level with the table with a large area to the left of the machine to support the quilt. Machine quilt on a day when you are relaxed to help avoid muscle strain down your neck, shoulders, and back. Sit in a raised stenographer's chair so your arms can rest on the table.

"Stitch in the Ditch" to Anchor Rows and Borders

1. Thread your machine with matching thread or invisible thread. If you use invisible thread, loosen your top tension. Match the bobbin thread to the backing.

2. Attach your walking foot, and lengthen the stitch to 8 to 10 stitches per inch or 3.5 on computerized machines.

3. Roll quilt widthwise to the center. Clip the roll in place. Slide the roll into the arm of your sewing machine.

4. Spread the seams open, and "stitch in the ditch."

5. Unroll the quilt to the next row. Clip the roll in place, and "stitch in the ditch."

6. Continue to unroll and roll the quilt until all the seams are stitched, anchoring the blocks.

Free Motion Stitch in the Ditch

The easiest way to quilt around the Angel, Main Street buildings and blocks is by free motion machine quilting around each piece either "in the ditch" or ¼" away. If you are a novice at this technique, imperfections are easily hidden

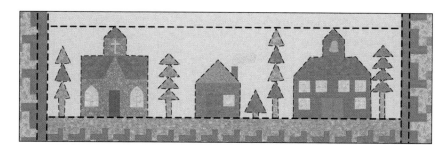

by using invisible thread and "stitching in the ditch." Use a darning foot and drop or cover feed dogs with a plate. No stitch length is required as you control the length. Use a fine needle and a little hole throat plate with a center needle position. Use invisible or regular thread in the top and regular thread to match the backing in the bobbin. Loosen the top tension if using invisible thread.

1. Bring the bobbin thread up on the edge of the block or applique, or ¼" away. Lower the needle into the background fabric and drop the foot. Moving the fabric very slowly, take a few tiny stitches to lock them. Snip off the tails of the threads.

2. With your eyes watching the outline of the block or shape ahead of the needle, and your fingertips stretching the fabric and acting as a quilting hoop, move the fabric in a steady motion while the machine is running at a constant speed. By moving the fabric underneath the needle side to side, and forward and backward, outline the shape of the Angel and other blocks. Lock off the tiny stitches and clip the threads at the end.

Free Motion Stippling

Free motion stippling is an overall meandering design to fill in the background around the "stitch in the ditch" outlines. Because it is "free form," marking is not necessary. The machine set up and technique are the same as free motion "stitch in the ditch" quilting.

Set up a practice swatch of three layers to become comfortable with moving the fabric to make your desired size stitch. Adjust the tension for either invisible or regular thread. Practice moving your hands back and forward and sideways, but not turning the swatch.

Carol Selepec quilted this Town Square with a long arm professional quilting machine.

Adding the Binding

Use a walking foot attachment and regular thread on top and in the bobbin to match the binding.

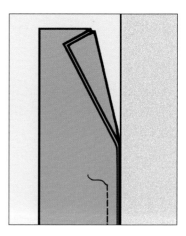

1. Square off the selvage edges, and sew 3" strips together lengthwise.

2. Fold and press in half with wrong sides together.

3. Line up the raw edges of the folded binding with the raw edges of the quilt in the middle of one side.

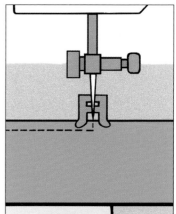

4. Begin stitching 4" from the end of the binding. Sew with 10 stitches per inch, or 3.0 to 3.5.

5. At the corner, stop the stitching ¼" from the edge with the needle in the fabric. Raise the presser foot and turn the quilt to the next side. Put the foot back down.

6. Stitch backwards ¼" to the edge of the binding, raise the foot, and pull the quilt forward slightly.

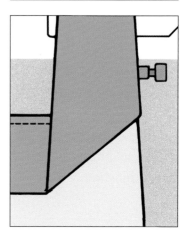

7. Fold the binding strip straight up on the diagonal. Fingerpress the diagonal fold.

8. Fold the binding strip straight down with the diagonal fold underneath. Line up the top of the fold with the raw edge of the binding underneath.

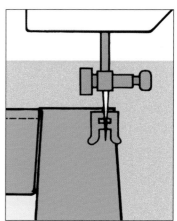

9. Begin sewing from the edge.

10. Continue stitching and mitering the corners around the outside of the quilt.

11. Stop stitching 4" from where the ends will overlap.

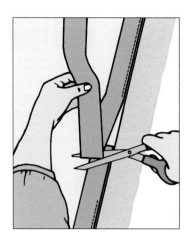

12. Line up the two ends of binding. Trim the excess with a ½" overlap.

13. Open out the folded ends and pin right sides together. Sew a ¼" seam.

14. Continue to stitch the binding in place.

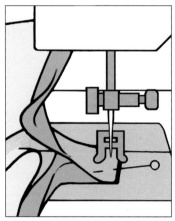

15. Trim the batting and backing up to the raw edges of the binding.

16. Fold the binding to the back side of the quilt. Pin in place so that the folded edge on the binding covers the stitching line. Tuck in the excess fabric at each miter on the diagonal.

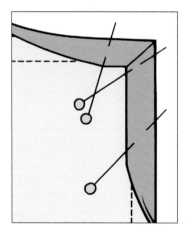

17. From the right side, "stitch in the ditch" using invisible thread on the front side, and a bobbin thread to match the binding on the back side. Catch the folded edge of the binding on the back side with the stitching. Optional: Hand stitch binding in place.

18. Sew identification label to back side.

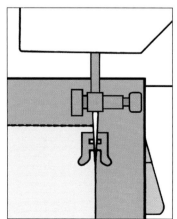

Aunt Edna's Quilt

Cutting for 20 Pinwheels and 22 Four Patches

Medium or Dark
(10) ¼ yd pieces
Cut strips from each for
total number given.

 Pinwheels
  (10) 1½" half strips

 Four Patches
  (8) 2½" half strips

 Sawtooth Edge
  (74) assorted 4" squares

Background
1½ yards

 Pinwheels
  (5) 1½" strips

 Four Patches
  (4) 2½" strips

 Setting Squares
  (4) 4½" strips cut into
   (30) 4½" squares
  (2) 7" strips cut into
   (6) 7" squares
  (2) 3¾" squares

Backing
1 yard

Batting
36" x 40"

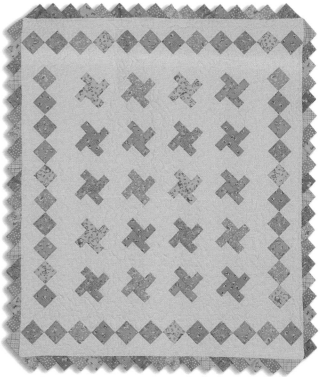

Eleanor Burns   *Finished Size: 33" x 39"*

Making Twenty Pinwheels

1. Follow Steps 1 through 13 on pages 25 – 27. Make two identical Pinwheels from each half strip, or mix them.

2. Sew a total of twenty Pinwheels.

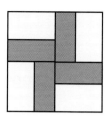

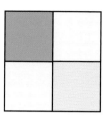

20 Pinwheels *22 Four Patches*

Making Twenty-two Four Patches

1. Follow Steps 1 through 8 on pages 22 – 23. Sew a total of twenty-two Four Patches.

Setting Top Together

1. Lay out the Pinwheels on point in rows four across and five down.

2. Fill in with (30) 4½" Background Squares.

3. Place Four Patches around outside edges.

4. Cut (6) 7" squares into fourths on both diagonals. Place around outside edges.

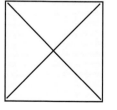

5. Cut (2) 3¾" squares in half on one diagonal. Place at corners.

6. Sew blocks into rows. Sew rows into top.

Making Sawtooth Border

1. Fold 4" squares on one diagonal, wrong sides together. Press.

2. Fold a second time on diagonal, and press.

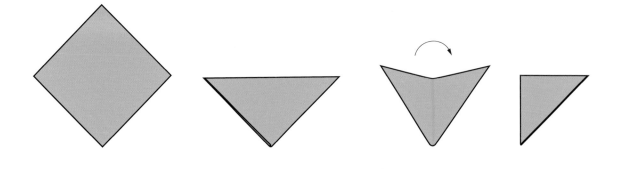

3. Place first folded Sawtooth at corner of quilt with raw edges matching raw edges of quilt. Anchor with ⅛" seam. Open, and center tip of second Sawtooth on first. Continue with ⅛" seam, evenly inserting folded Sawtooths around the outside edge of the quilt. You need approximately (19) for the long sides, and (16) for the short sides.

4. Adjust placement of Sawtooths at corners.

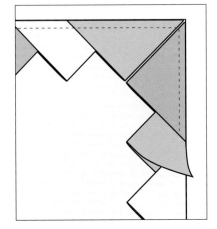

Quick Turning Quilt

1. Lay Backing out flat, right side up.

2. Place quilt top right sides together to Backing with Sawtooth Border tucked between the two layers. Pin layers together around the outside edge.

3. Stitch around outside edge, leaving an 18" opening in the middle of one side.

4. Place quilt on top of Batting, and trim Batting to size. Whipstitch Batting to edge of quilt.

5. Turn right side out.

6. "Stitch in the Ditch" around the Pinwheels and Four Patch. Stipple around the patchwork.

Maple Leaf Curtains

These directions are written for a curtain with two separate pieces. You may wish to make your curtain in one long piece.

Use for two-fabric or scrappy leaves

 Background 1¼ yds
(1) 6" strip cut into
    (6) 6" squares

(1) 3" strip cut into
    (12) 3" squares

(3) 2½" strips cut into
    (12) 2½" squares
    (14) 2½" x 6½"

(3) 2½" strips
(3) 6" strips

 Dark for Stems ⅛ yd
(2) 1" strips

Sue Bouchard   *Each curtain finishes at 12½" x 50"*

Two-Fabric

 Dark Medium ⅓ yd
(1) 6" strip cut into
    (6) 6" squares

(2) 2½" strips for Border

 Light Medium ⅓ yd
(2) 2½" strips cut into
    (36) 2½" squares

(2) 2½" strips for Border

 Backing
1½ yards

Scrappy Leaves

 **Six Fabrics** ¼ yd each
(1) 6" square from each
(6) 2½" squares from each
(1) 2½" x 25" from each

Making Twelve Leaves

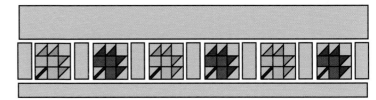

1. Make twelve Leaves following instructions on pages 30 – 34. Divide into two rows of six, one for each half of curtain.

2. Sew two rows together with 2½" x 6½" Background strips between each block, and beginning and end of each row.

3. Piece 2½" and 6" Background strips into two long strips.

4. Sew 2½" strip to bottom of each row, and 6" strip to top of each row.

Making the Rainbow Border

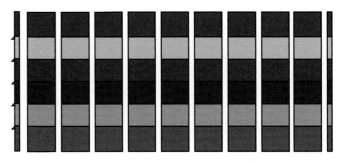

1. Sew 2½" x 25" Leaf fabric strips together lengthwise. Press seams to one side.

2. Cut into (9) 2½" segments, and sew end to end into one long strip.

3. Cut two Rainbow Borders the same length as the curtains. Pin and sew to the bottom of curtains.

Finishing the Curtains

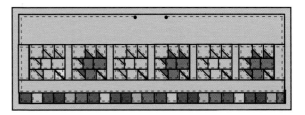

1. Cut backing in half along the fold to make two pieces 21" x 54". With right sides together, place patchwork curtain on backing fabric.

2. Sew ¼" seam all the way around the outside edge, leaving a 6" opening in the middle of the top. Trim backing to curtain.

3. Turn right side out. Check that there are no pleats along the seams. Press. Slipstitch the opening shut.

4. Fold the top 6" strip in half toward the back so the top edge extends ¼" lower than the seam on the front side. Pin.

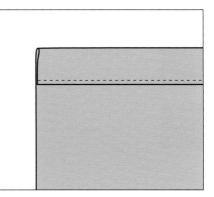

5. Stitch in the ditch from the front side. Press crease in top of curtain.

Fall Harvest

Eleanor Burns *Finished Size: 38" x 51"*

 Background 1⅛ yds

Twelve Leaves
- (6) 6" squares
- (12) 2½" squares

Twelve Stems
- (12) 3" Background squares

Divider Strips
- (7) 3" strips cut into
  - (6) 32" strips
  - (8) 3" x 5½" pieces
  - (15) 1½" x 6½" pieces

- (2) 2" strips cut into
  - (24) 2" squares

 First Dark Leaves
(3) 6" squares

First Medium Leaves
(18) 2½" squares

Second Dark Leaves
(3) 6" squares

Second Medium Leaves
(18) 2½" squares

 Leaf Stems
(2) 1" strips

 Pumpkins
(6) 5½" x 7" rectangles

 Pumpkin Stem
(1) 7" square

 Fusible Interfacing
(1) 7" square

 Folded Border ¼ yd
(5) 1¼" strips

 Border
(4) 5" strips

Batting
42" x 54"

Backing
1⅝ yds

 Binding ½ yd
(5) 3" strips

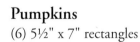

130

Making Leaves

1. Make six Leaves from First Dark and First Medium following instructions on pages 30 – 34. Make six Leaves from Second Dark and Second Medium.

2. Sew three rows of four Leaves each with 1½" x 6½" Background dividers between each block, and at the beginning and end of each row.

3. Sew 3" x 32" Background strips to top of each row. Trim strips even with blocks.

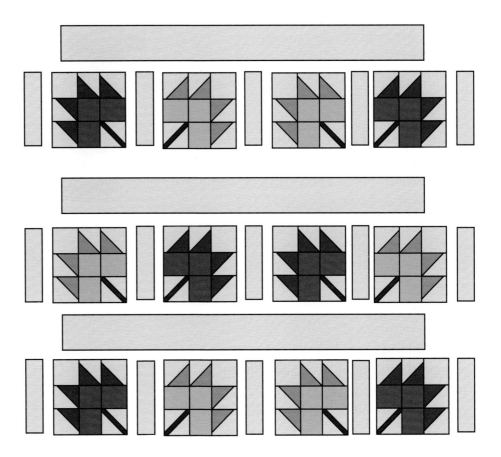

Making Pumpkins

1. Draw diagonal lines on wrong side of (24) 2" Background squares.

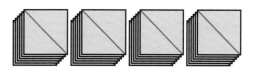

2. Place 2" squares on corners of Pumpkin rectangles, right sides together. Sew on lines.

3. Trim ¼" from lines. Press seams toward Background.

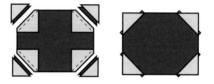

4. Sew two rows of three Pumpkins each with 3" x 5½" Background dividers between each block, and at the beginning and end of each row.

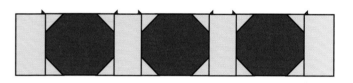

5. Sew 3" x 32" Background strips to top of each row. Trim strips even with Maple Leaf rows.

6. **Stems:** See pages 58 – 61 for Applique instructions. Trace six Stems on smooth side of interfacing. Place fusible side of interfacing against right side of stem fabric. Sew on the lines, trim, and turn.

Full Size Stem

7. Position Stems on Pumpkins, fuse, and sew.

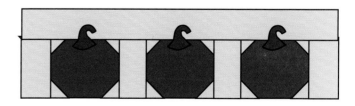

Finishing Quilt

1. Lay out five rows and sew together.

2. Sew 3" Background strip to bottom of quilt. Trim strip.

3. **Folded Border:** With wrong sides together, press 1¼" strips in half lengthwise. Match raw edge of Folded Border to raw edge of quilt. Using 10 stitches per inch, sew Folded Border to two opposite sides of quilt with seam slightly less than ¼". Do not press out. Sew Folded Border to top and bottom of quilt, overlapping in corners.

4. Pin and sew 5" Borders to quilt, and trim even with quilt.

5. Machine quilt and bind.

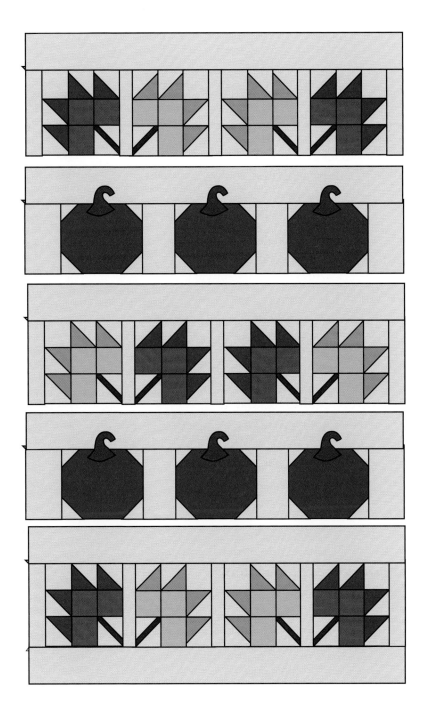

Duck and Ducklings

Lap Robe

Background 3 yds
Pieced Squares
(1) 6" strip cut into
(7) 6" squares

Small Triangles
(4) 2½" strips cut into
(52) 2½" x 3¼" pieces

Interior Lattice
(6) 2½" strips cut into
(48) 2½" x 4½" pieces

Setting Squares
(2) 10½" strips cut into
(6) 10½" squares

Side and Corner Triangles
(2) 15½" strips cut into
(3) 15½" squares
(3) 8" squares

Border
(5) 2½" strips

Loretta Smith   *Finished Size: 50" x 64"*

Different Mediums
Pieced Squares
(7) 6" squares

Large Triangles
(2) 4½" x 5¼" rectangles
of 13 different fabrics

Center Squares
(12) 2½" squares

Border ½ yd
(5) 2½" strips

Binding ½ yd
(5) 3" strips

Backing and Batting
58" x 72"

Grandmother's Choice

Lap Robe

Background 3 yds
Small Triangles
(4) 3¼" strips

Interior Lattice
(6) 2½" strips cut into
(48) 2½" x 4½" pieces

Setting Squares
(2) 10½" strips cut into
(6) 10½" squares

Side and Corner Triangles
(2) 15½" strips cut into
(3) 15½" squares
(2) 8" squares

Border
(5) 2½" strips

Medium 2 yds
Corner Squares
(4) 2½" strips

Large Triangles
(4) 4½" strips cut into
(26) 4½" x 5¼" rectangles

Center Squares
(1) 2½" strip cut into
(12) 2½" squares

Border
(5) 2½" strips

Binding ½ yd
(5) 3" strips

Backing and Batting
58" x 72"

Sue Bouchard   *Finished Size: 50" x 64"*

Duck and Ducklings Lap Robe

1. Following page 38, make 52 pieced squares from seven sets of 6" squares.

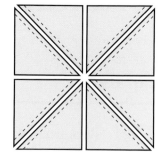

2. Sew to 2½" x 3¼" rectangles. Keep like fabrics together. Sew pairs together.

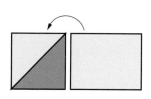

3. Pair patches with (26) 4½" x 5¼" rectangles.

4. Make 52 Corner Patches following directions on pages 39 – 41. Set four Corner Patches aside for Borders.

5. Sew 48 remaining Corner Patches into twelve blocks.

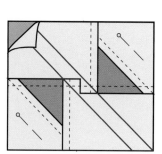

Make 26

Set 4 aside for Borders

Grandmother's Choice Lap Robe

1. Following page 44, sew four sets of 2½" Medium and 3¼" Background strips. Cut (26) 2½" pairs and sew together.

2. Following page 40, place 2½" pairs right sides together with (26) 4½" x 5¼" rectangles.

3. Make 52 Corner Patches. Set four Corner Patches aside for Borders.

4. Sew 48 remaining Corner Patches into twelve blocks.

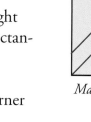

Make 26

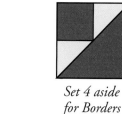

Set 4 aside for Borders

Finishing Either Quilt

1. Measure blocks. They should measure 10½" square. If they differ, cut six Background Setting Squares to that measurement.

2. Lay out twelve blocks on point in rows of three across and four down.

3. Place six Setting Squares in center of layout.

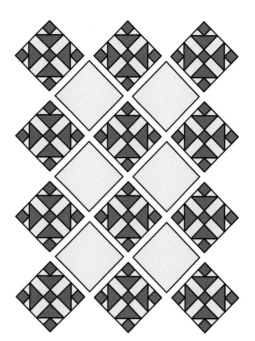

4. Cut three 15½" Background squares on two diagonals. Place around sides, top, and bottom of quilt.

5. Cut two 8" Background squares on one diagonal. Place in four corners.

(3) 15½" squares

(2) 8" squares

6. Sew top together. Straighten outside edges.

7. Piece 2½" Border strips, and sew into one long strip.

8. Cut four strips the same size as the top.

9. Sew Borders to sides of quilt.

10. Sew four Corner Patches to top and bottom Borders. Sew Borders to quilt.

11. Machine quilt and bind.

Stars of Friendship

Tablerunner

 Background ½ yd
Points
    (2) 4" strips

Corners
    (2) 3½" strips cut into
        (20) 3½" squares

 Star Points ⅓ yd
(2) 5" strips

Star Center Squares ⅛ yd
(5) 3½" squares

 Side and Corner Triangles ½ yd
(1) 14" strip cut into
    (2) 14" squares
    (2) 7½" squares

 Folded Border ¼ yd
(5) 1¼" strips

 Border 1⅛ yds
(6) 6" strips

Binding ½ yd
(5) 3" strips

Backing and Batting
28" x 76"

Placemat

One Star Block

 Borders ¼ yd
    (2) 4" x 9½" strips
    (2) 3" x 17" strips

 Binding ¼ yd
(2) 3" strips

 Backing and Batting
16" x 19"

Teresa Varnes   *Placemat: 14" x 17" Finished Size*
Tablerunner: 24" x 72"

Rectangular Tablerunner

1. Following pages 48 – 55, make five stars and sew together with side and corner triangles.

2. **Folded Border:** With wrong sides together, press 1¼" strips in half lengthwise.

3. Match raw edges of Folded Border to raw edges of Tablerunner. Using 10 stitches per inch, sew Folded Border to two opposite sides of Runner with seam slightly less than ¼". Do not press out. Sew Folder Border to top and bottom overlapping in corners.

4. Piece Border strips together, and sew to sides. Press seams toward Border. Sew Borders to top and bottom.

5. Quilt and bind.

Pointed Tablerunner:
Make Stars and sew together with side triangles. Eliminate 7½" squares cut on one diagonal for corners.

Placemat

1. Sew 4" Borders to sides of Star block. Press seams toward Border. Square Borders with sides.

2. Sew 3" Borders to top and bottom. Press seams toward Border. Square Borders with sides.

3. Quilt and bind.

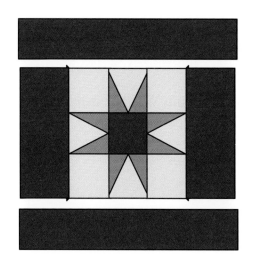

Guardian Angel

Wallhanging

 Dress and Sleeve
(1) 6" x 12"

 Dress Bottom
(1) 3½" x 6"

Dress Lace
6" of lace 1" wide

 Hair
(1) 3" x 6"

 Halo
3½" square

 Wing
6" x 10"

 Head, Hands, Feet
3" x 8"

 Sky ⅔ yd
(1) 21" square

 Trees
(4) different 9" x 12" pieces

Medium Weight Fusible Interfacing
1 yd

 Ground ¼ yd
(1) 8" strip

 Directional Borders 1 yd
(1) 5" Top strip (cut parallel to selvage)
(2) 5" x 21" Side strips (cut selvage to selvage)

Patricia Knoechel   *Finished Size: 30" x 32"*

 Or Non-Directional Borders ⅓ yd
(2) 5" strips

 Folded Border (Optional) ⅛ yd
(2) 1¼" strips

 Binding ⅜ yd
(4) 3" strips

 Batting and Backing
1 yd of each

Embellishments
Garland
   (15) ½" ready-made ribbon roses
   or (10) ½" gold star buttons with shank

¾ yd cording

(5) ½" gold star buttons for Tree Tops

3" Hair Garland

1. Select the left Angel. Trace selected pattern pieces on smooth side of fusible interfacing. Patterns are in the back of the book.

2. Make one Angel following instructions on page 58.

3. Trace a set of one large, one medium, and one small tree for each 9" x 12" piece of fabric for a total of twelve trees. Patterns are on page 83. Sew, trim, turn, and stuff.

4. Arrange Angel pieces on 21" Sky piece 3" down from top edge. Allow room for the Garland.

5. Fuse Angel pieces in place.

6. Sew outside edges of Angel by hand or machine. Leave tips of Hands unsewn.

7. Sew optional Folded Border.

For a variation, make a dark sky with white ground and trees.

8. Sew 5" x 21" Side borders to Angel, and then 5" Top Border.

9. Sew 8" Ground strip to bottom of Angel.

10. Arrange Trees and fuse in place. Sew outside edges.

11. Arrange Garland. Tack ends of Garland under Hands. Sew or glue Garland, silk flowers, and star buttons in place.

12. Quilt and bind.

Patricia Knoechel   *Finished Size: 30" x 32"*

Tooth Fairy Pillow

 Dress and Sleeve
(1) 6" x 12"

 Dress Bottom
(1) 3½" x 6"

 Dress Lace
6" of lace 1" wide

 Hair
(1) 3" x 6"

Halo and Basket
(2) 3" to 4" doilies

Wing
6" x 10"

 Head, Hands, Feet
3" x 8"

 Sky 1 yd
   Pillow Front
     (1) 19" square

   Pillow Back
     (2) 10" x 19"

Medium Weight Fusible Interfacing
   ½ yd

2⅛ yds ready-made piping

18" square Pillow Form

20" square Batting

Patricia Knoechel   *Finished Size: 18" square*

Embellishments
Assortment of 5 to 6 ready-made ribbon roses

6" of ¼" gold cording for Wand

1½" gold Star applique

3" Hair Garland

6" of white cording for Basket Handle

Tiny Pearls (optional)

Making the Angel

1. Trace all pattern pieces for left Angel on smooth side of fusible interfacing. Patterns are in the back of the book.

2. Make one Angel following the instructions on pages 58 – 62. Omit halo.

3. Arrange Angel pieces on 19" Sky piece, allowing room for Wand and Basket.

4. **Halo:** Arrange smaller doily under head. Tack with stitches or tiny pearls.

5. Fuse Angel pieces in place.

6. **Basket:** Fold doily in half and place with Handle lightly touching Hand.

7. **Wand:** Insert end under second Hand. Stitch or glue in place.

8. Sew outside edges of Angel by hand or machine. Tack ends of garland under Hair.

9. Sew bottom edge of Basket only. Glue Handle and silk flowers in place using washable fabric glue.

Finishing the Pillow

1. Center pillow top on batting and machine quilt ¼" from Angel.

2. Apply piping around outside edge with zipper foot. Clip for rounded corners.

3. Hem 19" sides of Backing pieces.

4. Place right sides together to pillow front, overlapping hems in the center. Pin.

5. Sew around outside edge with zipper foot. Trim batting to edge of piping.

6. Turn right side out, and stuff with pillow form.

Save the Trees

Wallhanging

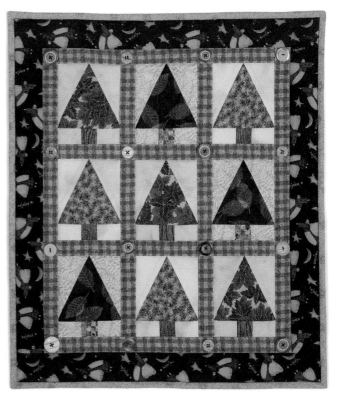

Patricia Knoechel   *Finished Size 20" x 23"*

Three Greens ¼ yd of each
(1) 5" x 12" of each

Three Backgrounds ⅛ yd of each
(4) 3" x 6" of each
(2) 2" x 5" of each

Three Browns ⅛ yd of each
(1) 1½" x 5" of each

Lattice ¼ yd
(4) 1½" strips cut into
    (6) 1½" x 5½"
    (4) 1½" x 16"
    (2) 1½" x 21"

Border ¼ yd
(2) 2½" strips

Binding ¼ yd
(3) 2¾" strips

Backing ⅔ yd

Batting
23" x 26"

Buttons
(16) ¾" to 1"

Triangle in a Square Rulers

or Templates for 4½" Triangle in a
Square, page 14.

144

Making Trees

Make three Trees from each of the three sets for a total of nine Trees. See pages 73 – 76 for more information.

1. **Background:** Layer (4) 3" x 6" Background rectangles in two pairs wrong sides together. This step is essential for mirror image pieces.

2. Layer cut on one diagonal. Sort triangles right side up.

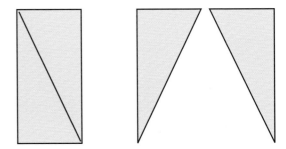

3. **Green:** Layer (3) 5" x 12" green pieces right side up. Cut three triangles using Triangle Ruler or template. Accurately line up narrow part of triangle with strip.

4. Lay out Green triangles with Background triangles, right side up. One Background set is extra.

5. Sew together.

6. Square to 4½".

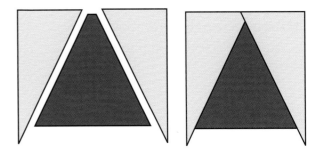

7. **Trunks:** Sew 2" x 5" Background strips to 1½" x 5" Trunk strip. Press seams toward Trunk.

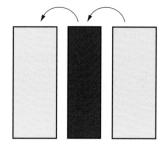

8. Cut (3) 1½" x 4½" pieces from each set.

9. Sew Trunks to Trees. Press seams to Trees.

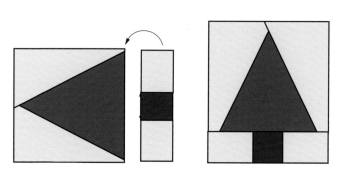

Sewing Top Together

1. Arrange Trees in three rows of three. Alternate colors as in photo.

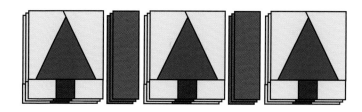

2. Place 1½" x 5½" Lattice strips between Trees. Stack and assembly-line sew.

3. Clip rows apart, and press seams toward Lattice. Sew (4) 1½" x 16" Lattice strips to rows. Trim ends.

4. Sew rows together, carefully lining up vertical seams. Press seams toward Lattice.

5. Sew 1½" x 21" Lattice strips to sides. Press seams toward Lattice. Trim ends.

6. Add 2½" Borders to sides, top, and bottom.

7. Machine quilt and bind. Sew on buttons.

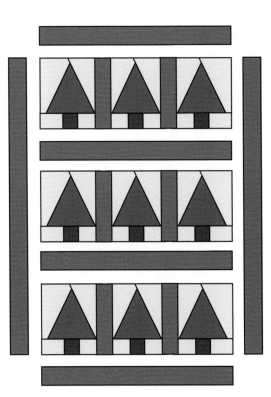

Teresa Varnes   *Finished Size 20" x 23"*

Angels on High

Wallhanging

Angels
Cut as listed on page 57

Sky 1⅛ yd
(1) 18" strip
(1) 6" x 18" piece
(2) 4½" squares
(1) 3¼" x 10½"
(1) 4" x 10½"
(1) 5" x 15"

Ground and Trees ½ yd
(1) 8" strip
(1) 8" x 10" piece

Church
Cut as listed on page 85
Omit (1) 3" x 16½" Sky strip

Cottage
Cut as listed on page 91 Omit Sky

School
Cut as listed on page 99

Folded Border ⅛ yd
(3) 1¼" strips

Top and Side Borders ½ yd
(3) 4½" strips

Binding ½ yd
(5) 3" strips

Batting and Backing
50" x 55" of each

Patricia Knoechel   *Finished Size: 44" x 50"*

Embellishments
Garland
1 yd cording
(14) ½" ready-made ribbon roses
or (12) ½" gold star buttons with shank

Angel's Hair
6" Hair Garland
(2) silk ribbon roses

Wreaths
1 yd decorative trim

Making Main Street

1. **Church:** Sew according to directions on pages 86 – 89. Leave off 3" x 16½" Sky strip on right side of Church. Trim from bottom so Church is 16" high.

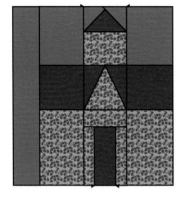

2. **Cottage:** Sew according to directions on pages 92 – 95. Sew 3¼" x 10½" Sky strip to left side. Sew 4" x 10½" Sky strip to right side. Sew 5" x 15" Sky strip to top. Square to 14" wide x 16" high by trimming from top and right sides.

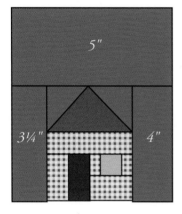

3. **School:** Sew according to directions on pages 100 – 104. Sew 3" x 16½" Sky strip to right side. Trim from the bottom so School is 16" high.

4. **Wreaths:** Cut into 4½" pieces. Center and hand sew into each Window.

5. Sew three buildings together.

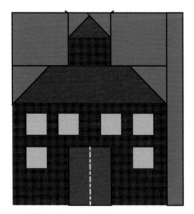

6. Sew the 6" x 18" Sky piece to the 18" Sky strip. Trim this piece to the length of the assembled buildings.

Making Angels and Trees

1. Sew two Angels according to directions on pages 58 – 62.

2. Trace and sew one medium and three small Trees from Ground fabric. Patterns are on page 83.

3. Center Angels on 18" Sky strip 5" down from top. Allow 9" open space between Angels.

4. Fuse Angels and sew in place. Leave tips of Hands unsewn.

5. Pin and sew Angel strip to Main Street.

Adding Folded Border

1. Sew (3) 1¼" strips into one long strip. Press seams open.

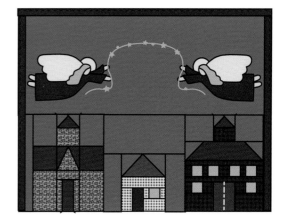

2. With wrong sides together, press in half.

3. Matching raw edges, sew to two opposite sides with 10 stitches per inch, and a seam slightly less than ¼". Do not press out.

4. Sew Folded Border to top of Wallhanging, overlapping in corners.

Adding Side and Top Borders

1. Sew 4½" strips to two opposite sides with 10 stitches per inch.

2. Press out, and square ends.

3. Piece Top Border, and sew to Wallhanging.

4. Piece 8" Ground strips, and sew to bottom of Wallhanging.

5. Position Trees between buildings. Fuse and sew in place.

6. Machine quilt and bind.

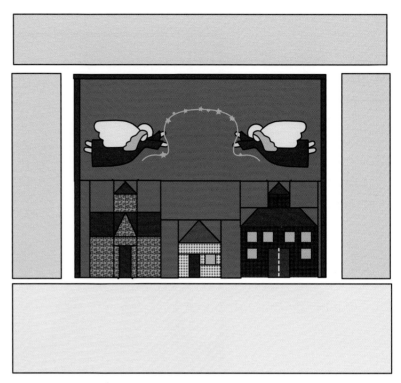

Arranging Garland

1. Arrange Garland, and tack ends under Hands.

2. Sew or glue Garland, silk flowers, or Star Buttons in place.

Quilt Show

Wallhanging

Patricia Knoechel   Finished Size: 35" x 47"

Angels
Cut as listed on page 57

Sky 1 yd
   (1) 18" strip

Spacers
   (1) 3½" x 10½" piece
   (2) 4½" x 10½" pieces
   (1) 8½" x 10½" piece

Roof
   (2) 4½" squares for each Cottage

Three Cottages
Cut as listed on page 91 except Sky

Folded Border ⅛ yd
(3) 1¼" strips

Grass ⅜ yd
(2) 6" strips

Trees
(4) 5" x 9" pieces

Top and Side Borders
Non-Directional ⅓ yd
Directional 1½ yds
(3) 3½" strips

Binding ½ yd
(5) 3" strips

Batting and Backing
38" x 50"

1. Sew two Angels following instructions on pages 58 – 62. Center Angels on one 18" Sky strip. Allow 8" between Angels for Yo-yo Garland. See Garland instructions on pages 68 – 71.

2. Make three Cottages according to instructions on pages 92 – 95.

3. Sew Cottages together with Sky spacers.

4. Sew Cottage Row to Angel Row. Trim sides.

5. Sew Folded Borders, Sides, and Top Border to three sides.

6. Piece together 6" Grass strips. Sew to bottom of Wallhanging. Square sides.

7. **Trees:** Make one large, one medium, and two small Trees. Fuse Trees between Cottages.

8. **Little Quilts:** Cut two 3½" x 3" pieces from fabric that resembles miniature quilts. Place right sides together to backing fabric. Sew around outside edge, leaving a small turning hole at top. Turn right side out. Slip stitch opening shut. Tie a string for Clothesline from Cottage to Large Tree, and sew quilts to string.

9. Machine quilt and bind.

Teresa's Church

Wallhanging

Church
Cut as listed on page 85 except Sky

Sky ¼ yd
(2) 2½" squares
(1) 4" x 16½"
(1) 5" x 16½"
(1) 3½" x 21"
(2) 4½" x 5½"

Dark Stairs ⅛ yd
(1) 6" x 2" Top of Stairs
(4) 6" x 1¼" pieces

Medium Stairs ⅛ yd
(4) 6" x 1" pieces

Folded Border ⅛ yd
(2) 1¼" strips

Border ⅓ yd
(2) 3½" strips

Green Trees
(3) 9" x 12" pieces

Teresa Varnes   *Finished Size: 29" x 26"*

Fussy Cut Flowers
(2) 3" squares

Stained Glass Windows
(3) 3½" x 5" pieces

Ground ¼ yd
(1) 7" strip

Fusible Interfacing
⅔ yd

Clover Fusible Bias Tape
1 yd

1. Make Church following directions on pages 86 – 89. Add 4" x 16½" Sky piece to right side of Church, 5" x 16½" Sky to left side, and 3½" x 21" Sky to top.

2. Straighten edges.

3. Add Folded Border to three sides of Church.

4. Sew Border to three sides.

5. **Stairs:** Begin with the dark 2" x 6" step. Sew strips together, alternating medium and dark strips. Press seams toward Top Step. Cut a piece of fusible interfacing 6" x 7". Place dotted fusible side of interfacing right sides together to Stairs. Make marks at top 1½" in on each side. Make marks at bottom ½" in. Draw lines between the two marks. Sew on the lines, trim, and turn.

6. Fuse Stairs to center of 7" Ground strip, and center under Door. Pin and sew to Church. Square sides.

7. **Trees:** Trace two large, two medium, and three small Trees on smooth side of the fusible interfacing. Sew, trim, and turn. Patterns are on page 83.

8. **Stained Glass Windows and Cross:** Make one Cross and three Windows. Patterns are on page 106. Fuse to Church. Press fusible bias tape to inside and outside of Windows.

9. **Fussy Cut Flowers and Trees:** Fuse and stitch appliques in place.

10. Machine quilt and bind.

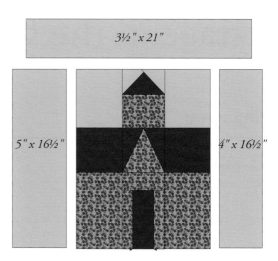

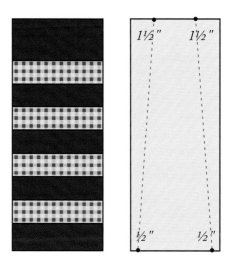

Cottage in the Country

Wallhanging

 Sky ¼ yd
(1) 5" x 10½"
(1) 3½" x 10½"
(1) 2" x 17"
(2) 4½" squares

 Cottage, Chimney, and Smoke
Cut pieces according to page 91

 Ground ¼ yd
(1) 5½" x 22"

 Trees
(4) 5" x 9" pieces

 Sidewalk
(1) 6" square

 Fussy Cut Flowers
(2) 3½" squares

 Folded Border ⅛ yd
(1) 1¼" strip

 Checked Border ¼ yd
(2) 3½" strips

 Backing and Batting
24" square

 Binding ¼ yd
(2) 2¾" strips

Medium Weight Non-woven
Fusible Interfacing ½ yd

Lace for Curtain 4"

Patricia Knoechel   *Finished Size 19" x 21"*

Making the Cottage

1. Sew lace to Window. Make the Cottage following directions on pages 92 – 95.

2. Starting from the top, sew the 3½" x 10½" Sky piece to the right side of the Cottage, and the 5" x 10½" Sky piece to the left.

3. Sew the 2" x 17" strip to the top. Square outside edges.

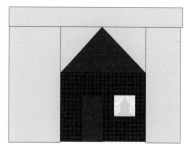

Adding the Folded Border

1. With wrong side together, press 1¼" strip in half lengthwise.

2. Match raw edge of Folded Border to raw edge of Cottage.

3. Using 10 stitches per inch, sew Folded Border to two opposite sides of Cottage with seam slightly less than ¼". Do not press out.

4. Sew Folded Border to top of Cottage, overlapping in corners.

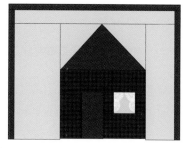

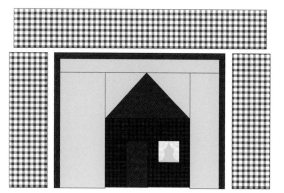

Adding the Checked Border

1. Pin and sew Borders to two sides. Press seams toward Border.

2. Pin and sew Border to top. Press seam toward Border.

Finishing the Wallhanging

Follow applique instructions for sewing, trimming, and turning on page 58.

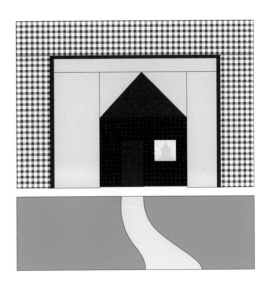

1. Trace Sidewalk on smooth side of non-woven fusible interfacing. Pattern is on next page. Sew sides only, trim, and turn.

2. Line up 5½" x 22" ground strip under Cottage, position Sidewalk, and fuse in place.

3. Center Sidewalk under Door, and sew Ground strip to Cottage. Press seam toward Ground. Stitch Sidewalk in place.

4. Place fusible side of interfacing right sides together to Flowers fabric.

5. On wrong side of fabric, draw outline of flowers with permanent marking pen, and sew on lines. Trim and turn.

6. Trace one large, one medium, and two small Trees on smooth side of fusible interfacing. Patterns are on page 83. Sew, trim, and turn.

7. Position Trees and Flowers around Cottage. Fuse and stitch in place.

8. Quilt and bind.

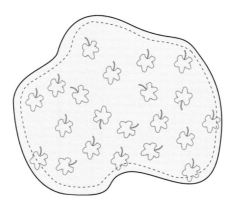

Patricia Knoechel   *Finished Size 19" x 21"*

Fussy Cut villagers are from Carol Endres line of fabric called Market Square, manufactured by Benartex, Inc. Fussy Cut instructions are on page 105.

Full Size Sidewalk Pattern

Amber's Schoolhouse

Wallhanging

 School
Cut all pieces on page 99 except Windows and 3" x 16½" Sky

 Sky ½ yd
  Spacers
    (1) 5" x 25"
    (2) 3½" x 4½"
    (1) 1½" x 16½"

  Trunks
    (1) 2" strip cut into
      (2) 2" x 21"

  Trees
    (1) 5"strip

 Trunks
(1) 1¼" x 21" strip

 Trees
(3) 4" x 12" pieces different greens

 Blue Four Patches ¼ yd
(3) 2½" strips

 Red Four Patches ¼ yd
(3) 2½" strips

Edna's Pinwheel ⅛ yd
(2) 1½" strips

Amber Varnes   *Finished Size: 32" Square*

 Ground ¼ yd
  Edna's Pinwheel
    (2) 1½" strips

  Row Dividers
    (2) 2½" strips

 Binding ⅓ yd
    (4) 3" strips

Backing and Batting
36" square

White Pima Cotton for Windows
9½" x 12" piece

Making Photo Transfers for Schoolhouse Windows

1. Select six of your favorite classmate photos. Faces should fit into a 2" square. Photos can be reduced or enlarged in size when transferred.

2. Place tape on the back side of each photo. Tape all six to one master sheet, leaving at least 1" between each photo.

3. Take to a copier that can copy the photos onto photo transfer paper. Transfer the photos with mirror image.

4. Place photos right side down against the Pima cotton.

5. Apply heat to back side of photo transfers according to manufacturers directions. Do not apply steam.

6. Center and cut each photo into a 2½" square.

Amber is the 11-year-old pictured in the top left corner of the school. She designed and made the wallhanging.

Making Schoolhouse

1. Make Schoolhouse, following directions on pages 100 – 104.

2. Sew photos in Window positions.

3. Sew 1½" x16½" Sky piece on left. Press seam toward Sky.

4. **Do not square up.**

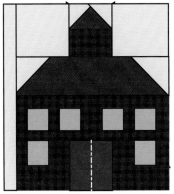

Block should measure 16½" x 15½".

Making Trees

1. Make three Triangle in a Square Trees, following instructions on pages 74 – 76. Cut five pairs of 2½" x 5" rectangles from the Sky on one diagonal and ten 4" triangles from Tree fabric.

2. **Trunks:** Sew 2" Sky strips to 1¼" Trunk strip. Press seams toward Trunk. Cut into two 3½" and one 4½" piece.

3. Sew Trees together according to illustration. Trim Trunks to match width of Trees.

4. Sew Trees to each side of Schoolhouse from top to bottom.

5. Sew 5" x 25" Sky strip to top. Square with Trees.

Making Eighteen Four Patches

1. Make eighteen Four Patches following the instructions on pages 22 – 23.

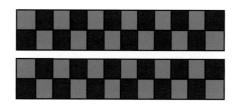

18 Four Patches

2. Divide into three stacks of six Four Patch each. Sew one set together for Top.

3. Sew remaining two stacks for Sides. Note that the Sides are mirror image to the Top.

4. **Top:** Center, pin and sew right sides together to top of Schoolhouse.

5. **Side Borders:** Matching top blocks, pin and sew to sides of Schoolhouse.

6. Trim bottom of Schoolhouse and Trees to length of Side Borders.

Making Eight Pinwheels

1. Sew two 1½" Pinwheel and Ground strips right sides together.

8 Pinwheels

2. Make eight Pinwheel blocks following the instructions on pages 25 – 26.

3. Sew Pinwheels together into one row.

4. Pin and sew Row Dividers to top and bottom of row.

5. Press seams away from Pinwheels.

6. Pin and sew to bottom of Schoolhouse.

7. Square outside edges.

8. Quilt and bind.

Split Rail with Geese

Queen Size Quilt

 Background 5½ yds

Split Rail Blocks
(18) 2" strips

Flying Geese Blocks
(6) 7" strips cut into
    (36) 7" squares

Setting Squares
(7) 6½" strips cut into
    (40) 6½" squares

Side Triangles
(2) 10"strips cut into
    (7) 10" squares
(2) 5½" squares for Corners

First Border
(3) 2½" strips for Top and Bottom
    (4) 2" strips for Sides

Third Border
  (8) 3½" strips

 Medium or Dark
(18) ¼ yd pieces cut into
    (1) 2" strip from each for Split Rail
    (2) 5½" squares from each for Geese

 Fourth Border 2 yds
(10) 7" strips

Teresa Varnes   *Finished Size: 82" x 108"*

 Binding 1 yd
(10) 3" strips

 Backing 6½ yds
Cut into (2) equal pieces

 Batting 90" x 116"

Making Fifty-Four Split Rail Blocks

1. Make three identical Split Rail Blocks from each 2" medium or dark strip sewn together with a 2" Background strip. Follow instructions on pages 113 – 115.

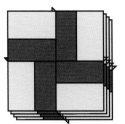

54 Split Rail Blocks

2. Make a total of 54 blocks. The blocks should measure 6½". If your blocks measure other than 6½", cut your Setting Squares to that same measurement.

Making 142 Geese

1. Make four identical 2½" x 4½" Flying Geese from each 5½" medium or dark square sewn together with a 7" Background square. Follow instructions on pages 78 – 79.

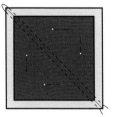

2. Make a total of 142.

3. Assembly-line sew two sets of 40 Geese each for Side Borders.

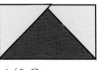

142 Geese

4. Assembly-line sew two sets of 31 Geese each for Top and Bottom Borders.

Setting Top Together

1. Lay out the Split Rail blocks on point in rows six across and nine down.

2. Fill in with (40) 6½" squares.

3. Cut (7) 10" squares into fourths on both diagonals. Place around outside edges.

4. Cut (2) 5½" squares in half on one diagonal. Place at corners.

5. Sew blocks into rows. Sew rows into top.

6. Straighten outside edges.

7. Piece together 2" First Border strips and sew to Sides. Square ends. Press seams toward Border.

8. Piece together 2½" First Border strips and sew to Top and Bottom. Square ends. Press seams toward Border.

9. Pin and sew 40 Geese strips to Sides. Press seams away from Geese.

10. Pin and sew 31 Geese strips to Top and Bottom. Press seams away from Geese.

11. Piece and sew remaining Borders to quilt top.

12. Quilt and bind.

6½" squares
cut 40

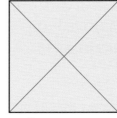

10" squares
cut 7

5½" squares
cut 2

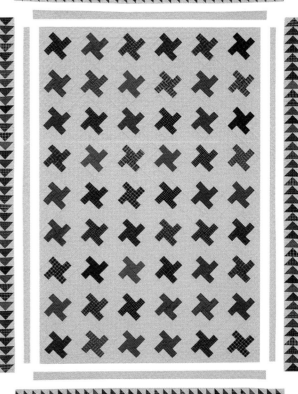

Split Rail with Geese

Lap Robe

 Background 1½ yds

Split Rail Blocks
(8) 2" strips

Flying Geese Blocks
(5) 7" strips cut into
 (25) 7" squares

 Setting Squares ⅔ yds
(3) 6½" strips cut into
 (15) 6½" squares

 Second Background 1½ yds

Side Triangles
(1) 10"strip cut into
 (4) 10" squares
(2) 5½" squares for Corners

First Border
(3) 2½" strips for Sides
(2) 2" strips for Top and Bottom

Third Border
(6) 3½" strips

 Medium or Dark
(8) ¼ yd pieces cut into
 (1) 2" strip from each for Split Rail
 (3) 5½" squares from each for Geese
 (1) 5½" square from one Geese

 Binding 1 yd
(6) 3" strips

Teresa Varnes   *Finished Size: 52" x 68"*

Following Queen size directions on pages 165 – 166, make a total of 24 Pinwheels and 100 Geese. Sew 27 Geese together for sides, and 23 Geese for top and bottom.

 Backing 3½ yds
Cut into (2) equal pieces

Batting
58" x 74"

167

Split Rail

Lap Robe

Teresa Varnes   Finished Size: 46" x 62"

Split Rail Background 1 yd
(8) 2" strips

Split Rail
Medium or Dark ⅛ yd each of eight
(1) 2" strip from each

Setting Squares ⅔ yd
(3) 6 ½" squares cut into
   (15) 6½" squares

Side and Corner Triangles ½ yd
(4) 10" squares
(2) 5½" squares

Framing Border ¼ yd
(5) 1¼" strips

Border 1⅛ yds
(6) 6" strips

Backing 2¾ yds

Batting
50" x 68"

Sewing 24 Blocks Together

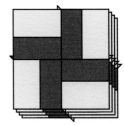

1. Make three identical Split Rail Blocks from each 2" medium or dark strip sewn together with a 2" Background strip following instructions on pages 113 – 115. Make a total of 24 blocks.

2. Lay out in rows four across and six down.

3. Fill in with (15) 6½" Setting Squares.

4. Cut (4) 10" squares into fourths on both diagonals. Place around outside edges.

5. Cut (2) 5½" squares in half on one diagonal. Place at corners.

6. Sew blocks into rows. Sew rows into top.

7. Straighten outside edges.

8. Sew Framing Border and Border to four sides.

9. Quilt and bind.

Straight Rails Quilt

 First Dark ½ yds
(8) 2" strips

 Medium 1 yd
(16) 2" strips

 Second Dark ½ yd
(8) 2" strips

Framing Border ¼ yd
(5) 1½" strips

 Border 1 yd
(6) 5" strips

 Binding ⅝ yd
(6) 3" strips

Backing 3 yds

Batting
52" x 64"

Teresa Varnes   *Finished Size: 47" x 59"*

Sewing 48 Blocks Together

1. Following instructions for the Split Rail
   Border on pages 113 – 115, make 48 blocks.

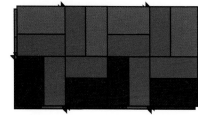

48 Blocks

2. Sew into 24 pairs.

3. Count out eight stacks of three pairs each.

4. Sew into eight rows with three pairs each, or six
   blocks in each row.

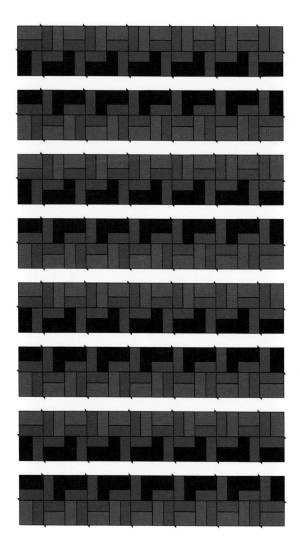

24 Pairs

5. Lay out rows, alternating placement every
   other row.

6. Sew top together.

7. Sew 1½" Framing Borders and 5" Borders on
   four sides.

8. Quilt and bind.

Index

Order Information

Quilt in a Day books offer a wide range of techniques and are directed toward a variety of skill levels. If you do not have a quilt shop in your area, you may write or call for a complete catalog and current price list of all books and patterns published by Quilt in a Day®, Inc.

Easy

Make a Quilt in a Day Log Cabin
Irish Chain in a Day
Bits & Pieces Quilt
Trip Around the World Quilt
Heart's Delight Wallhanging
Scrap Quilt, Strips and Spider Webs
Rail Fence Quilt
Flying Geese Quilt
Star for all Seasons Placemats
Winning Hand Quilt
Courthouse Steps Quilt
Nana's Garden Quilt
Double Pinwheel
Easy Strip Tulip

Applique

Applique in a Day
Dresden Plate Quilt
Sunbonnet Sue Visits Quilt in a Day
Recycled Treasures
Country Cottages and More
Creating with Color
Spools & Tools Wallhanging
Dutch Windmills Quilt
Grandmother's Garden Quilt

Intermediate

Trio of Treasured Quilts
Lover's Knot Quilt
Amish Quilt
May Basket Quilt
Morning Star Quilt
Friendship Quilt
Kaleidoscope Quilt
Machine Quilting Primer
Tulip Quilt
Star Log Cabin Quilt

Burgoyne Surrounded Quilt
Snowball Quilt
Tulip Table Runner
Jewel Box
Triple Irish Chain Quilts
Bears in the Woods

Holiday

Christmas Quilts and Crafts
Country Christmas
Bunnies & Blossoms
Patchwork Santa
Last Minute Gifts
Angel of Antiquity
Log Cabin Wreath Wallhanging
Log Cabin Christmas Tree Wallhanging
Country Flag
Lover's Knot Placemats
Stockings & Small Quilts

Sampler

The Sampler
Block Party Series 1, Quilter's Year
Block Party Series 2, Baskets & Flowers
Block Party Series 3, Quilters Almanac
Block Party Series 4, Christmas Traditions
Block Party Series 5, Pioneer Sampler
Block Party Series 6, Applique in a Day
Block Party Series 7, Stars Across America

Angle Piecing

Diamond Log Cabin Tablecloth or Treeskirt
Pineapple Quilt
Blazing Star Tablecloth
Schoolhouse Quilt
Radiant Star Quilt

Quilt in a Day®, Inc. • 1955 Diamond Street • San Marcos, CA 92069
1 800 777-4852 • Fax: (760) 591-4424 • www.quiltinaday.com